Untold Stories from Boyle Heights

An
IN OUR GLOBAL VILLAGE
Book

Untold Stories from Boyle Heights

An
IN OUR GLOBAL VILLAGE
Book

BY CLASS OF 2011 SENIORS
SCHOOL OF LAW AND GOVERNMENT
ROOSEVELT HIGH SCHOOL
LOS ANGELES, CALIFORNIA

Copyright © 2011 School of Law and Government at Roosevelt High School

All rights reserved.

No part of this book may be reproduced, in any form, without written permission from School of Law and Government at Roosevelt High School, Los Angeles, California

Book design by Steve Mereu, Karen Cerezo, Marissa Medina, Michelle Lira, and Eddie Ruiz

Manufactured in the United States of America

ISBN-13: 978-0615476919

ISBN-10: 0615476910

School of Law and Government, Roosevelt High School, 456 South Mathews Street, Los Angeles, CA 90033

Contents

Leticia's Quince *Ismael Aguiar*	1
A Mother's Everlasting Love *Reina Aguirre*	3
My Preterm Labor *Wendy Aguirre*	6
Alma's Story *Aracely Alvarado*	9
Road Trip *Xochilt Alvarez*	11
A Family Struggle *Jesus Arellano*	13
My Grandfather *Arturo Banda*	15
The Lonely Years *Melanie Barajas*	18
La Candelaria *Allan Bautista*	22
Life Of A Single Mother *Rebecca Baxter*	25
The Decision *Alejandro Berumen*	27

Never The Same *Juan Carbajal*	29
To Reunite A Family *Magdalena Ceja*	31
Brief Memories *Karen Cerezo*	35
A Discovered Talent *Omar Cruz*	38
Negative To Positive *Michelle Duran*	40
Innocence *Leslie Escobedo*	42
A Teenage Pregnancy *Agustin Esparza*	45
One Special Dance *Denise Felix*	48
An Unforgettable Day *Michael Fernandez*	51
Born To A Big Change *Edgar Garcia*	53
Family Man *Isabel Garcia*	55
Building Success *Stephanie Gonzales*	58
Maternal Love *Miguel Hernandez*	61
The Loss Of A Child *Justo Juarez*	63

Crazy Situations *Michelle Lira*	65
Journey To America *Nancy Lopez*	70
A Pregnant Story *Nicholas Manriquez*	73
Summer Love *Alyssa Medina*	75
The Speech Is Toe-Day *Marissa Medina*	78
Three Days *Oscar Mojica*	80
Family Left Behind *Lesly Molina*	82
Innocence Taken Away *Betty Morales*	85
A Struggle For Change *Jesus Oropeza*	87
Great Expectations *Angelica Ortega & Elizabeth Farfan*	89
Summer Days In Boyle Heights *Hector Ortega*	93
Success Of A Dream *Georgina Portillo*	96
A Bad Superstition *Julio Prado*	99
The Path *Maribel Ramon*	101

The Lack Of A Better Future *Anthony Romo*	104
An Immigrant's Dream *Adriana Salas*	108
A Ticket To America *Michelle Salinas*	111
My Dad's Dream *Abraham Sanabria*	114
David's Memories *David Sanchez*	117
A Physical And Emotional Struggle *Juan Sibrian*	119
A Mother's Struggle *Eduardo Simental*	121
The Surprises Of Life *Esthefanie Solano*	124
Always Remember *Joseph Torres*	128
A Road Of Sadness *Cristian Umanzor*	131
Story Of A Young Woman *Maria Uriostegui*	135
9 Months *Brenda Valadez*	137
A Mother's Journey *Luis Valencia*	140
Abdon's Childhood *Hortencia Valenzuela*	142

The Road To Education *John Vargas*	145
American Dream *Miguel Vargas*	147
Remembering The Old Times *Edgar Velez*	150
Story Of A Girl *Ignacio Zermeno*	153
Our Hopes And Dreams	156

Preface

These untold stories were written by Class of 2011 Seniors at the School of Law and Government. Following in the tradition set the previous year with our first In Our Global Village book, *Boyle Heights Through the Eyes Of Its Youth*, this year's class chose to tell the stories of their parents and family members, and in the process gave voice to those that often go unnoticed. Unlike last year's project, these chapters were constructed by individual students, who interviewed their subjects countless times in order to tell true stories of the past.

Although each story possesses a unique and distinct voice, many of them share similar themes, involving birth and death, hardship and determination, home and dislocation, love and cruelty, family and independence. Through their literary portraits, this year's seniors captured their loved ones as they see them, as they are. For some students, this project provided an opportunity to sit down for the very first time and learn of their family members' past. Others encountered the harsh reality of struggling with communication and of relationships that need mending.

To the seniors who were brave enough to delve deeply into these stories, we hope that you remember all of the interviews, all of the drafts, but especially the experience of learning more about the loved ones around you.

For the reader, we hope that you read these stories without

judgment and that the diversity and strength of the Boyle Heights community emerges from the pages. These stories are important and real. This is the young generation demanding that they be passed on.

- Leticia Rojas, Jeffrey Matsumura, Steve Mereu
School of Law and Government
Roosevelt High School, Los Angeles, California
May 2011

Leticia's Quince

ISMAEL AGUIAR

It was exactly one week until Leticia's birthday. As the days went by, she grew unsure if her quinceañera was going to happen. A girl's quinceañera is a ceremony that is held on the girl's fifteenth birthday. This ceremony is the passing of a girl into a woman.

Leticia became more and more worried her family wasn't going to celebrate her fifteenth birthday. Thoughtful and very caring, her oldest sister Christina made a call to her aunt, whose nickname was "Chona." As time went on, Leticia began to doubt her birthday was going to be celebrated. What she didn't know was that her aunt had gathered all of Leticia's aunts and uncles. Her Aunt Chona was planning a surprise birthday party for her beloved niece. Leticia was unaware that this was going on. Throughout the week, preparations were being made for the event, but Leticia knew nothing about it.

At fourteen years old, Leticia was very caring. As a middle child, she took care of her younger siblings in a family of twelve. She was

Leticia

very cheerful and very helpful and didn't expect anything back from others.

The only people who knew about Leticia's birthday celebration were her aunts, uncles, parents, and her oldest sister. One day her sister Christina took measurements for Leticia's dress. But Leticia didn't think it was for her fifteenth birthday. She was very confused as that was going on. When the special day arrived, all of her family came together to celebrate. The celebration took place at her childhood home in Tijuana. There was no expensive catering, just the typical rice, beans, tortillas and chicken. Although the whole thing wasn't very expensive, it was a very memorable celebration. Leticia remembers standing in front of all her guests and seeing everyone who came together to make that day a special one for her.

Leticia remains the same woman she was in the past, caring more for others and not worrying much about herself. From a young age she had to take on the role of a mother to help her own mother raise her younger siblings.

A Mother's Everlasting Love

REINA AGUIRRE

Juana Flores lived in a small house in the enormous city of Leon, Guanajuato, in the center of Mexico. In that small house, Juana and all her brothers and sisters grew up together without a mother. At the young and vulnerable age of eight, Juana experienced the tragedy of losing her mother. Without her beloved mother, Juana grew up without the knowledge that a growing girl should have received from her mother.

One night in 1979, Juana, her mother, father, brothers, and sisters sat on the front porch of their home talking and drinking some delicious *Jicama* her dad had brought home from his plot of land. After a while, Juana's mother told everyone to go to sleep. It was very late at night. As usual, Juana's older brother, Francisco, hadn't come home yet. Her mother waited until he got home to give him some dinner. Early the next morning, Juana's mother felt ill. Without hesitation, Juan (Juana's father) and Rosa (Juana's sister) took Juana to the hospital. Meanwhile, without knowing the condition of their beloved mother, Juana, together with her sisters and brothers, went to school. When Juana was heading home after school, she heard from one of her neighbors that her mother was terribly ill. When she heard the terrible news, Juana ran to her house. When she arrived home she noticed that her mother wasn't there. Her father and older sister had already taken her to the hospital.

~

After a few hours, Juan returned from the hospital to leave Juana and her siblings under a neighbor's care while he returned to the hospital to check on his wife. After a few hours, tired and stressed, Juan returned to take his kids home. As soon as they walked into their house, Juan received a call from the doctor saying that his wife's condition had worsened. Quickly, he headed to the hospital leaving his children under the care of their aunt. Noticing that everyone at the house had worried faces, Juana felt a sense of despair for her mother's health.

Juana cried and cried because she wanted to see her ill mother, but everyone seemed to ignore her plea. After a while, Juana heard that her father had taken her mother to her sister's house. As soon as she heard that her mother had left the hospital, Juana ran as fast as she could to her aunt's house. In fact, everyone ran to the house. With everyone surrounding the house, Juana had no choice but to crawl through their feet to see her mother. When she saw her mother, her face whitened in horror as she witnessed her mother's appearance.

A couple of hours later, Juana's mother seemed to get worse. Noticing no improvements, everyone decided to take her to a bigger hospital. When her hospital ride arrived, her husband and a few of her children, including Juana, went with her. When Juana got in the car, she grabbed her mother's weak hands and sat on her legs. With her final breaths, her mother told Juana that everything was going to be alright. When she couldn't hear her mother's voice any longer, Juana looked up to see her face. She wouldn't speak and her eyes stared in one direction. With intense sadness, Juana cried for her mother and was held by her older brother who took her out of the car so she wouldn't see what was happening.

A few days later, Juana and everyone else in the family fell into an abyss of depression. Juana's older brothers, Rafael and Francisco, always fought each other while Juana and her two older sisters took charge of cleaning the house, doing the chores, preparing the food, taking care of the baby, and going to school. Sadly, Juana's father Juan fell into such a deep depression that he started drinking and became an alcoholic. He drank to fill the deep gap caused by the loss of his beloved wife. Sometimes, his children would look for him at night when he didn't return home.

A few months after the passing of his beloved wife, Juan realized that getting drunk would not bring his wife back. His children also helped him by telling him how much he meant to them and how they didn't want to also lose their father. Thanks to those love-filled words, Juan raised his eight children like his wife would have wanted, with love.

My Preterm Labor

WENDY AGUIRRE

She will never forget all of the planning and waiting. Her first attempt at conceiving was unsuccessful. She ended up in a deep depression. At last, her second attempt was successful. She tried not to be anxious, so she waited a few days after her missed period to test. She nervously waited to see the two little lines that would prove if she was pregnant or not. At the sight of both lines, she felt relief, but also nervousness at the memory of her stillborn child three months earlier.

Two months later at the hospital, a little flicker of the baby's heart showed everyone that the baby was alive and doing well. Not only did that flicker of light show that she had life blooming inside of her, it also showed the hardship that would soon come. It wasn't easy for her and her husband to keep the news hidden from their families, but the idea of becoming parents themselves actually began to sink in. After letting everyone know about the pregnancy, she started to plan.

To begin, she wanted to know the gender of the baby in order to start thinking of what to get it. She also wanted to paint their room according to the gender of the baby, to begin getting the feeling of motherhood.

Unfortunately, during the pregnancy she still had to work under stressful conditions. The supervisor didn't seem to understand that she wasn't able to perform the same as before due to the baby she had to carry. She continued to push carts full of office supplies, move boxes of old binders, and constantly had to move up and down from her seat. It was a constant battle, one that she wasn't meant to win.

At twenty-two weeks into the pregnancy, she went into pre-term labor. The night before she was admitted to the hospital, she felt that something wasn't right. Nervously, she made the decision to tell her supervisor that she wasn't feeling good and had to leave to see the doctor. She was admitted to the doctor's office immediately and after doing an internal, the doctor sighed, "Oh boy." The doctor told her she would be back and left immediately. When the doctor came back, she calmly told her to get dressed and move to the hospital as quickly as possible, as they were expecting the baby to be born soon. The doctor told her to transfer to the hospital because she was in active labor, and was two centimeters dilated.

The baby was coming, and fast! Luckily, the doctor's office was located next to the hospital where she was to deliver the baby. Frantically, she called her husband many, many times but couldn't get in touch with him, so instead she got a few of her co-workers to call for her to tell him the news of the baby's early arrival. The only person she succeeded at contacting was her mother, who came rushing after hearing the news. At the moment, she had thoughts of having the baby alone. Soon, she was in a delivery room attached to a heart rate monitor. The doctors began to ask her how she felt about having the baby. She was scared at the thought of having the baby alone. While she lay in bed, having contractions every two to three minutes, her husband and mother arrived, right before she was transferred to another room. The doctors gave her a large dose of medicine to stop the contractions. She broke into sweats, started vomiting, and began to have blurred vision. The contractions stopped. On the fifth day, she was sent home.

At thirty weeks, something unexpected happened -- her water broke. Soon after, the contractions began and she, her husband, and her mother quickly left for the hospital. The pain was so bad, everyone thought she would give birth in the car. Minutes later, at the hospital, she was taken to the delivery room. The contractions began to increase rapidly, with force. She knew at that moment she would give birth in that room. About four hours later, filled with pain, she gave birth to a baby. Thirty weeks into the pregnancy, she gave birth to a healthy and wonderful baby girl that weighed five pounds. After a week at the hospital, she and her baby left for home. The feeling of being a mother for the first time overflowed in her, and still does.

Alma's Story

ARACELY ALVARADO

Alma Martinez grew up near La Mirada, California, a conservative, quiet place where retired people relax. It has a sleepy feel to it. It is also a clean place where people can smell fresh cut grass. Alma Martinez, the youngest of five children, didn't see her father often while growing up. She always saw her parents struggle; her father came home with red eyes, tired from working as a busboy in a restaurant. Her mother worked in the strawberry fields in the extreme heat. Alma hated her father working such long hours but knew that he did it in order to provide a better life for his children. She realized that she didn't want to struggle like her parents. Their struggle inspired her to go to college to help her family with their money issues.

Alma

When Alma went to college, she joined MEChA (Movimiento Estudiental Chicano de Aztlan), a program that guided Latino/a youth to go to college and graduate. Through this program, she learned about the challenges that Latinos face, such as high drop-out rates, the difficulties of being undocumented students, and teen pregnancy. Alma believed that when one Latino kid dropped out of college, it was like one thousand Latinos dropping out of college. They only made up a small percentage of the students who attended college. She thought people needed to take care of each other and to look out for each other.

After Alma graduated with a Master's in Education, she wanted to give back to her community. After attending and graduating from USC, she wanted to share her experience to encourage other Latinas to attend a college or university and to graduate.

She was unemployed for six months because she wanted to find a job that was the "right fit." For a short while, she was offered a job in Boyle Heights. Her love for East Los Angeles is indescribable because she saw people with problems similar to her's. Her mission was to work with young women who had the potential to attend college and to empower them through the Latino culture. She happily thought this was an amazing program as she identified with the girls and the parents.

Next, she got a job with Strengthening Families, which helps families who are homeless or at-risk of becoming homeless. She addressed the needs of the East Los Angeles and Boyle Heights Latinos by providing them with the necessary tools to help them get back on their feet. She achieved her life's goal.

Road Trip

XOCHILT ALVAREZ

In 1998, Yolanda Alvarez experienced going on a trip to New Mexico. She went to a convention in Santa Fe, a city with open fields, where the sun shines brightly. In order to go on the trip, the parents of children in second to fifth grade had to volunteer hours at their school. She completed roughly one hundred hours in five months. Yolanda and the other parents couldn't wait for the day of the trip. They left for Santa Fe by train. Uncomfortable on the train, she couldn't wait to get off and stretch. It took one night for the group to get to Santa Fe and rest. Yolanda was excited to finally arrive, as it had been a long ride. After the train, she took a bus to Albuquerque, the place where she would stay for the remainder of the trip.

After Yolanda dropped off her belongings, she and the others went to dinner. Smelling the delicious food made her even hungrier. In the morning she woke up to the smell of coffee. Yolanda hurried and got dressed because they were visiting the Albuquerque Museum of Art and History.

The museum had exhibits about the city's origins as a Spanish colonial village, which gave her a whole new perspective on the place. The Albuquerque Museum of Art and History also included artworks in all traditions, from the works of indigenous peoples, to Spanish colonial art, to cutting-edge modern installations. Yolanda loved the art because some was decorated with dried chilis and ceramic art.

This reminded her of her home. She had never gone to a place where Native Americans still lived. They met indigenous students who were being taught in their language.

The streets and houses were made of adobe, which resembled Mexico, her native land. She had flashbacks of when she lived in Mexico. She hadn't been there in a long time and that's why she felt like a young kid again. Finally, Yolanda went to the Church of Beethoven where she watched the performances and listened to music. Yolanda was extremely thankful that she experienced the trip. To go on another trip again, she would be willing to complete one hundred hours.

A Family Struggle

JESUS ARELLANO

School and life have always challenged my mother, Letticia Guerra. In 1990, the sun shined brighter for Letticia while living in Boyle Heights. Letticia remembers her days as a Roosevelt High School student as the best years of her life. She radiated friendship to all who surrounded her. Letticia's friends admired her determination, hard work, and her ability to multi-task.

Letticia Guerra

Friday night dances were some of the best school events. The dances at Roosevelt High School had both positive and negative outcomes. Letticia enjoyed attending school events but fights and shooting also found their way into Friday night dances. Most of the dances at school involved violence. Letticia said it was always the troublemakers that caused and started the problems that ruined the night for the students. Still, this did not restrain her from socializing and getting involved.

She enjoyed the Oldies. All the couples began dancing romantically. There were many girls, but the cherry red hair and glossy black eyes of Letticia stood out the most and captivated most people.

After the dances, she and her friends went out to eat. They gathered at Jack-in-the-Box. At the restaurant my mom would ask herself why people would use violence to disturb the life of others. She wondered why they acted violently if violence never solved anything. Every time Letticia mentioned her thoughts to her friends they made fun of her for having those foolish ideas. They told her not to worry about the well-being of others and the negative actions they took. They told her to worry about her own well-being and the actions she took.

During my mom's high school years, violence surrounded her and made her life hard. Although not much has changed since her years at Roosevelt, many students look past the negativity of our school and walk blindly without acknowledging issues that affect our everyday lives. They decide to ignore these issues and pretend that they don't affect them.

Letticia was very proud that she never let violence affect her life. The violence she faced made her a stronger woman because she always fought for justice. Letticia Guerra is a wonderful, proud, strong woman.

My Grandfather

ARTURO BANDA

On the morning before his birthday, January 31, 1973, my grandfather, Cirilo Flores, made a decision to come to the United States because, at thirty years old, he was tired of living in poverty. He had difficult times in Mexico. For example, there were times when he did not have any food because there was no work, which meant no

Cirilo Flores with his wife

money. This made him feel awful because he knew his family could not eat. My grandfather tried different ways to make money and he went to different places to find work. He did not care what kind of work he found as long as it would pay. He lived in a very small house where there was nothing nearby: no schools, doctors, etc. That's why he decided to come to the U.S. -- to get a better life.

One morning he went to the rancho to see a coyote (a person who crosses people to the U.S. illegally) that his friend recommended. He told the coyote that he wanted to go to the U.S. and asked how much it would cost to go to Los Angeles, CA. The coyote told him it would cost him 1,200 dollars. Cirilo made the decision to cross the border to the U.S. He agreed to meet the coyote at a bus station the following Friday at 7:00 pm. Cirilo took a taxi and, when he arrived at the bus station at 6:30 pm, he saw his friend who was also going to the U.S. When the three got on the bus to Tijuana, Cirilo told his friend, "This is like an adventure because we are going to a new country." After a tense ride, they arrived at a house in Tijuana to rest. Around 11:00 pm, three big vans arrived to the house to take them to the desert. Soon, he would begin a new life, a life in the United States of America.

They arrived at the desert at 11:50 pm. At around midnight, they started their dangerous trek through the desert. He was scared because the desert was pitch black and he couldn't see his surroundings. The coyote soon told them the shocking news; they were going to walk for three nights and two days in order to reach California. Everyone would rest in the big trees and drink any water they could find. When someone got tired, the coyote would wait until they got some energy back. Cirilo suffered much on his journey to the U.S. due to exhaustion and the lack of water. Other people had similar experiences. Some of them got thirsty and drank dirty water to survive. Others couldn't walk anymore due to extreme exhaustion. Even though the situation was dangerous, the other people and the coyote tried to help them and not leave a single person alone in the desert to die a slow and painful death.

Finally, on a Monday night, they arrived in California. Luckily, Cirilo went to Los Angeles with his friend who had a family there that was able to help them. After a few days, Cirilo started working in a restaurant and he started sending some of his hard-earned money to his wife. Sometimes he called home because he missed his wife and the family he left in order to provide for them.

Cirilo used to say, "The old days were very hard because I didn't have much work, but right now life's different."

Now, he enjoys his new life because he does the things that he always wanted to do. For example, he bought a house for his family, and his children went to school to get a good education.

He also said, "Now it is easier to get work because the economy has changed so much."

His trip to the U.S. was difficult but life-changing because, even though he suffered much, his life is better, his family has a big house, and his children go to school to receive a good education.

Cirilo is a good person because he said, "The future of my family comes first before other things." He also said, "Some people have the same experience that I had because the old days were very hard." Cirilo never gave up because his family means so much to him that he would die for their safety and well-being.

The Lonely Years

MELANIE BARAJAS

Alvaro and his family

Alvaro Barajas' life changed completely after his mother decided to leave Mexico and come to the United States. She left behind her daughter and two sons. At age eight, my father was left alone and abandoned. That windy, stormy night became my father's nightmare. The screeching tires and fading tail lights became his last memory of his mother. His time in Mexico was a nightmare becoming reality. The mistreatment he received from his family caused him misery. The series of events that happened during his three lonesome, miserable, derelict years helped him become the father he is today.

Before leaving, she took Alvaro to her brother. During the first couple of weeks, life was not as hard as he thought it would be without his mother's protection. Slowly, that feeling began to fade away when his cousins began to abuse him, physically and verbally. School became the only place where he felt safe and comfortable. As time progressed, my dad's uncle told him to leave school early so he could deliver lunch to his uncles at the "potreros." My dad and uncle left school early and took them lunch, but they had to return home since they weren't allowed back in school. After three months, my dad and his brother began to cut school and go to work.

Working was not difficult for Alvaro since he was young and didn't tire quickly. Working without shoes or sandals challenged him. The dirt was filled with sharp pointy glass, razor-sharp rocks, and other harmful objects. Alvaro walked barefoot and worked thirteen hours a day. The materials penetrated deep into his feet, which caused his feet to blister. Although pain overcame his body, he knew he could not quit work or take a break. He wanted to act like an eight year old and enjoy his childhood, but the circumstances didn't allow him to.

One day before Alvaro left school, his teacher reminded him that the following day they would be taking a field trip to a lake. Alvaro was thrilled. For the fist time in months he would be able to visit a place other than school, home, or work. The following day my dad went to the lake. Splashing, swimming, and laughing, my dad forgot his responsibility. He got caught up at the lake with his classmates and for the first time in months he enjoyed being a kid again. He felt the fresh water on his face and smelled the aroma of wet grass and flowers.

When the trip ended, he returned home to find his uncle and cousins at home. Then it struck him. He had forgotten to bring them lunch. He apologized and told them he just wanted to have fun for once. His uncle forgave him but his cousins grew furious and outraged because they didn't eat lunch. When his uncle left the living room, my dad's cousins brutally beat him. They made him cry. They hit him until they grew tired. Every hit was like a painful stab. Slowly, my father walked to his bed and cried. He missed his mom and his brother, and his uncle just ran away from the beatings and mistreatment. My dad felt alone and unloved. He felt that no one cared for him and he longed for a kiss or a hug from his mother. The following day he didn't go to school and went straight to work to make up for his mistake. That weekend his uncle and cousins got drunk. They apologized to my dad and gave him money to make up for their mistakes. My dad gladly took the money and bought himself food because he was starving. His first year living without his mother in Mexico was only the beginning of the brutal years that followed.

Day in and day out he was mistreated by his cousins, and on the weekends they would feel pity and give him money. My dad realized his half-brothers and sisters neglected him and pretended he did not exist. His older half siblings worked, but not once did they offer to give him money, a call, a visit, or worry about buying him basic necessities. They pretended they did not know him because they did not want to be responsible for another person and spend money on him. His life became a routine: work every day, get hit by his cousins, and miss his family. For months, they mentally abused him. As the second year came to a close, my dad looked forward to Christmas.

His uncle told him he was receiving presents this year. As a nine year old kid, my dad grew anxious to see what he would be getting. The day came and when he opened his present his heart sank. Instead of receiving clothes or shoes, he got an ax. His aunt told him he got an ax because it would make his job easier. The following day, the family went to the annual Christmas celebration in Nayarit. No one ever missed this celebration. The ocean-like aroma, the bright blue sky, and the warm heat of the sun helped my father enjoy his evening at the beach, Playa Platanitos. As he swam around in the clear blue water, he noticed that his half-brothers from his dad's side were at the beach as well. He ignored them and continued playing on his own. Out of nowhere he felt someone tugging hard on his leg. He kicked and yelled to set himself free but no one heard. As he struggled to turn, he noticed it was his stepsister trying to drown him. He struggled and fought to set himself free. Her nails dug deep into his flesh, causing excruciating pain. No one came to his rescue. He thought about letting her drown him to end his misery, but he decided not to. He fought with her until he kicked her hard enough and she let go. As he stepped out of the water he saw the blood dripping from his leg. He wiped it off with sand and ran to the mountain rocks where he sat and cried to himself. At that very moment he felt like an orphan. No one cared to help him or noticed he had gone missing. His older siblings ignored him, his younger brother ran away, and his family was in the United States. He had no choice but to be strong and wait for his mom to come get him.

As time progressed, my dad began to get fed up with all the abuse. He grew tired of crying himself to sleep and feeling alone whenever he got beat up. He missed his family. He just wanted to leave. Then, on a night filled with black shadows, pouring stormy rain, just like the night his mom left, my father decided to run away. In his mind he did not want to get hit any more. He packed the few clothes he had and silently left that night. He tried to think of a place where he could go and finally found one -- the old stick house where he used to live with his mom. He got to the house and put his belongings in a dry corner since the rain was dripping into the house. All night long he cried, but the rain washed his tears away. As morning approached, my father continued to cry. Luckily, his aunt happened to pass by. She heard his soft cries and went in to see who was inside. My dad told her everything that was occurring with my uncle, and even her eyes began to water. She told my dad to take his things, and that he was going to live with her. After that day my dad's life changed. He still had to work because his aunt could not provide for him. But the mental abuse stopped. He no longer felt mistreated and unloved.

Finally, the day arrived. My grandma called to say she was going to pick him up. When my father's brothers heard the news they rushed to pick up my father. They bought him new clothes and shoes. They dressed him properly so his mother would believe they cared for him. The day my grandma sent for my father and uncle, my dad felt ecstatic. As my father crossed the border, he vowed to never leave his children unattended. He didn't look back to say good-bye to his stolen childhood.

La Candelaria

ALLAN BAUTISTA

Alberto and Maria

It was 1983 when Maria Felix and Alberto Bautista met each other in Candelaria, Hidalgo, Mexico. Maria, a short, compact woman with long hair and brown eyes, used to be a pre-kindergarten teacher in Candelaria. One Friday afternoon during her first days as an educator, she had to stay late at school to work. Alberto went to the school because he had to pick up some papers. He was a man with short hair, no mustache, and a beard. He had an athletic body because he practiced boxing at that time. Maria sold raffle tickets to raise money for her school. When Alberto saw her, he was mesmerized by her brown eyes immediately; he felt that she would be the perfect woman to marry him. Alberto decided to buy all her tickets. This is how my parents met each other.

After a few weeks they decided to start a relationship. They maintained their relationship for three years. Finally, they got married. During this period they faced many problems caused by Maria's godparents. Maria had grown up in their house and they disapproved of her maintaining a relationship with Alberto. During those three years they decided to keep their relationship a secret.

When they finally decided to get married, Maria made a decision to let her godparents know. The day before the wedding, her godparents immediately locked her in a room. At that moment, a nephew of her godparents came to their house. The godparents told her to serve their nephew. She took advantage of the situation, went to her room very quickly, and took her important, personal papers and put them in her pockets.

She escaped through the back door. She started to run into the corn fields. She kept running until she found her neighbor, a taxi driver who had the reputation of being a good person. He helped Maria by letting her stay in his house. She told him about her situation. He knew Alberto's aunt, and drove to her home to bring her back to see Maria. She told Alberto's aunt the whole story. Her body trembled. She feared that her godparents would do something to my father. She knew how horrible they could be. She asked Alberto's aunt if she could help her since Alberto was in possible danger. She worried that they would beat him or even kill him.

Alberto's aunt told her nephew of the circumstances my mother was in, and recommended that he get to the church in order to seek advice from the priest. Alberto did what his aunt told him to do. He told the priest all the details regarding the Maria issue. The priest told Alberto that he did not have to be concerned about it and should get prepared for the wedding. Alberto went home and the priest went to my mother's godparents' house with two other people. When the priest arrived at their house, he screamed out their names and told them that if they did something to Alberto or made an attempt to stop the wedding, he would not hesitate to call the authorities. He was not afraid to put them in jail. The priest slammed the door and left their house.

After that, he went to the taxi driver's house and told Maria what he had done. Then the priest took my mother to the church because she would be better off staying there with him. Maria, still trembling with fear, ended up sleeping in the church that night. She just wanted peace of mind and happiness. While Alberto couldn't stop thinking about her, his frustration increased because he couldn't visit her due to their traditions and beliefs. In their village, it was thought to be bad luck to see one's future wife the day before a wedding.

The next day, two women helped Maria get prepared for the wedding. She felt extremely anxious. When the time came, my mother walked with the priest, holding his arm. They walked slowly into the church as Alberto waited for her. When she grasped my father's hand, she finally felt safe and relieved. The wedding was perfect and everyone appeared happy, with smiles on their faces, despite the presence of police officers with guns in their hands, prepared to prevent any chaotic situation from breaking out. The crowd was anxious with the thought that Maria's godparents would show up and cause an unforgettable scene. However, they never showed up.

Maria and Alberto were happy that day. The wedding went off without a glitch or any drama.

Life Of A Single Mother

REBECCA BAXTER

Grandma Maria was married in America and in Mexico. She ended up filing for divorce in Mexico, and brought her two children back to America. They needed to adjust culturally. Her children had never lived in America. They had to deal with a new house, a new school, a new country, and learn a new language. On top of that, they had to deal with not being able to see their father very often.

Maria felt fortunate to be able to bring her kids to America. The worst part of adapting was learning how to be a parent in a new country. She didn't know anyone who had been single, so she was on her own. She didn't have friends because she had never been in the U.S. before. She didn't have a church, and many of her family members had passed away. This was all new territory. How could she be a mother and a father to her children when she had to be the provider as well? She didn't know how to do it all; it seemed so difficult. Her children struggled with a one-parent household and she didn't realize it at the time. They missed their father. They thought they were the only ones who had divorced parents. Even after they had been in the States for a while, they still had the impression that nobody else had divorced parents. It was hard for them to adjust.

Although their father had been reliable in paying child support, it still wasn't enough for them to live in California. Mario no longer had any marketable skills, and had been out of work for ten years.

She was at a loss. How was she going to support her children and take care of the things her husband normally took care of around the house? She went from a situation where she had always felt "in control" and just found herself floored, realizing how small she was in this huge world that required so much of a person, especially when she had the lives of her small children in her hands and felt the need to be a role model for them. They depended on her to nurture and guide them. She was overwhelmed and very scared. She wasn't sure how she was going to handle all of these things.

Soon she realized that she didn't need to take on everything herself. She wasn't alone. Getting back to the U.S. with her children was a miracle and she didn't even know it until years later. She found a wonderful church where she had a fantastic support system. They welcomed her like a family would. They supported and guided her and also gave her the tools she needed to live a better life.

She felt excited to be around other single parents who were also going to meetings at the church. Almost overnight she began to see a huge change in her children. They were happier and at first she didn't understand why. Then her daughter said one day, "Everyone in my class says they have parents who are also divorced. I'm not the only one anymore." This was a breakthrough for her and Maria. She had seen what the program did for her children, so she decided to stick with the adult classes for her children's sake. At the end of the ten weeks she saw a change in herself as well, enough for even the instructor to notice. It was shocking to her, as she didn't believe that it could affect her like that. She knew she had to stick with this program.

What she learned overall was how to be a friend to her ex-husband so he could be the father that her children needed. Her children still needed him regardless of how she felt towards him. This really helped her children cope with a single parent home and divorced parents.

The Decision

ALEJANDRO BERUMEN

Julia Duran emigrated to the U.S. in 1974. She was a married woman with a daughter, but she was not happy in her marriage. One night she wasn't able to sleep thinking about coming to the U.S. It was 3:30 a.m. She was awake. She began looking for a contact, a phone number that her friend had given to her last month. She had forgotten that she had put it under her bed.

Julia was desperate. She couldn't find the number and she was cold because her blue dressing gown didn't protect her. She lifted up the mattress. She found a bunch of papers that she used to keep there. She searched through all the papers, looking anxiously for the card. She shook the papers and a little yellow card fell out. She felt a bit happy because that was what she was looking for. It contained the number and name of the person that was going to help her cross the border.

At 4:00 a.m. she was dressed to leave, taking advantage of the fact that her husband wasn't home. Otherwise he wouldn't have let her go. It was a cold morning and she wore long socks, a black dress, a black and white sweater, and a wrap on her head. She was going to her daughter's house to say goodbye and to ask her for help. She needed her daughter, Sara, to make a call to those people who were going to help her cross the border. By 8:30 a.m., her daughter had already called the "coyotes" to pick her up. They said their good-byes. Both of them cried because it was the last time they were going to see each other for a while. Julia was sad because it was very painful to leave her daughter, even though her daughter was already married. By 9:30 a.m., the people who were supposed to pick her up arrived. Julia and her daughter gave each other a big hug. At noon, she was on her way with the coyotes to pick up some other people before heading to the border where she was going to meet up with another group of people who were also going to cross the border.

The weather was getting hot and they were picking up five more people before heading up to Tijuana, Mexico. It was almost 100 degrees. They were traveling in a three-row van. They went from one town to another in the hot weather. It took them all day to pick everyone up because those people lived far from each other. Three of them lived about one to two hours away from each other and the other two were about thirty to forty minutes from each other. Finally, at about 8:30 p.m., they made their way to Tijuana, Mexico. It was going to be a journey of about two or three hours on the road before they met with the rest of the group that was going to cross over to the U.S. At night they were going to stop and rest at hotels.

Julia has always hoped that she had made the right decision. She never regretted it. Even now, she doesn't have regrets. She is happier than ever.

Never The Same

JUAN CARBAJAL

It was early- to mid-October of 2008, somewhere around the time when the sun had just set for about two to three hours. A distant relative of the family who had kept contact had come to visit because he had run into some financial trouble. After a while of proper greetings and proper conversation, the relative asked Mother for a loan and, being the kind person Mother was, she was happy to oblige. As Mother walked into her room, her youngest son was playing video games on her TV. Mother looked into the file cabinet where she had kept emergency money for "just in case" situations. When Mother opened the envelope where she kept the money, she noticed that a large sum was missing. Mother's heart sank in her chest; she had a mixed feeling of anger, disappointment, and betrayal. She returned to the relative waiting in the living room and she gave him what little money she had left. A soon as the relative left, mother yelled at all three of her children. At first, the youngest child said nothing, but before he could scramble away, Mother grabbed his wallet and noticed that the large sum of money that was missing was inside.

The son knew what he was doing when he took the money, but that didn't matter to him. He was only interested in hanging out with his friends and buying things. Mother knew that hitting the child would accomplish nothing, but both she and her son knew that he would never be seen in the same way again. He had stolen more than

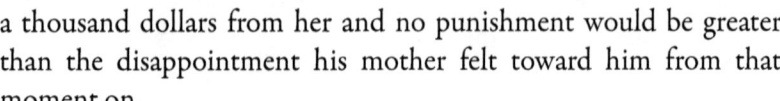

a thousand dollars from her and no punishment would be greater than the disappointment his mother felt toward him from that moment on.

To Reunite A Family

MAGDALENA CEJA

"What is your name?"
"Estella Camacho," she lied.
"Why did you cross?"
"I want to be with my husband," she replied, speaking the only honest words since the beginning of her questioning. The sounds of scribbling on a paper took her back to when the idea of crossing the border of Mexico was just that -- an idea.

Writing what would be her last words in the only country she had ever known, Maria explained to her husband her plan to reunite their family, a family divided by a border

Maria Elena Ceja

for five years. She scribbled on a sheet of paper, certainty in every word she wrote. In her final thoughts, she had but one last thing to write, "We either stay here with what we have or go over there (U.S.A.) together, but we have to stay as a family."

At eighteen and barely an adult, Maria Elena Ceja was already wed and a mother to three young children. In 1969, her husband, Benjamin, came to the United States from Mexico in search of work to provide a better future for his new family. Having found one, he knew he had to stay in the new country and try to communicate with his recently acquired family, a family so young but separated by poverty.

After five years of being apart, Maria grew weary of life without her husband and of her children's lives without a father. The dream of a family diminished with each passing day. She knew too many families around her had fallen apart. She would not let that happen to her own. So she decided to cross the border to keep the family together.

In order to succeed, Maria planned thoroughly. Benjamin's parents already lived in the United States and were willing to give her money to pay for the trip. However, with three children the journey became more difficult to complete. Therefore, with the help of her mother, Maria obtained documents belonging to another boy, already a citizen in the U.S., and used them to cross her oldest son Salvador (age 5) to the other side. With a final hug, my mother sent her child to what she knew would be a better future and promised him that they would soon reunite.

The night before her journey, Maria stayed with an aunt in Tijuana where she met with her husband's brother, Miguel, who would make the journey alongside her. Watching her baby daughters sleep, Maria prayed for a safe trip and finally shut her eyes, drifting to sleep.

October 10, 1973. Waiting for the moonlight, she gathered her belongings and reached for her daughter, trying hard not to disturb her peace. Holding her other daughter, Miguel made sure everything was in order with the crossing. The journey was dangerous, but worth the risk.

When the sunlight crept over the horizon, Maria's journey began. The truck driving her and Miguel to the border's fence awaited them. Finally arriving, the sight of the fence transmitted Maria's hopes as well as fears. Tightly carrying the babies, Maria and Miguel joined a fellow group of immigrants with similar plans. Besides Maria, only three other women walked in the group. Too frightened to talk to anyone, Maria kept to herself. Slowly approaching the fence, she didn't know what to expect. The cold night air sent shivers down her spine. Taking a deep breath, she jumped down a hole into a tunnel under the fence. The depth surprised her and caught her off guard. She lost her footing but quickly regained her balance. Crawling out, she sighed in relief when she saw Miguel and her baby had made it across safely.

Now on the other side, the sun arose on what was now a new life in a new home. Maria and Miguel walked to the house where they would stay until the "coyotes" (people who help immigrants cross the border for money) would pick them up to take them to the nearest city.

The next morning, Maria and Miguel's escorts picked them up. Riding through the dirt, she heard engines roaring at a distance. As quickly as she heard them, she saw another car racing down the road, followed by the border patrol. The border patrol failed to catch the racers but caught Maria, Miguel, and Maria's two baby girls.

While riding in the back of the border patrol van, they thought the ride would never end. The doors finally creaked open. Sunlight crept into the van, blinding Maria momentarily. Rushing out of the van, everyone was told to form two single file lines: men in one, women in the other. Frantically praying, Maria jumped at the sound of a man calling her into the room. Carrying one daughter and holding the hand of the other, she trudged inside. The authority politely asked her to sit. Surprising Maria, he gave her a warm smile and offered her children hot chocolate. Next, he proceeded with the questions known to many immigrants caught crossing the border.

"What is your name?" he asked.

"Estella Camacho," my mother lied.

"Why did you cross?" he continued.

"I want to be with my husband," she replied, speaking the only honest words since the beginning of her questioning. As he scribbled her words, she lost herself in her thoughts. She wanted to ask questions of her own. Where was Miguel? How long until she could go home? What will happen to her and her children? Quickly, she realized she shouldn't. Her thoughts abruptly came to a stop when the officer asked his next question.

"What is his name?" he questioned.

She lied again. She gave a make believe name. As the interrogation continued, Maria went through a series of emotions until it finished. They sent all of them to a detention center. She would have to return to Mexico, but her journey and the journeys of the others who were caught were not over. Maria never gave up her dream of reuniting her family. A year later, her dream came true. Perseverance and faith -- she thinks of these ideas every time she remembers this story. Perseverance and faith helped the "American dream" come true. Every time I hear this story, the same message plays in my head. Never give up on your dreams.

Brief Memories

KAREN CEREZO

Gerardo Cerezo Romero

I wish I knew more about my dad`s past but he doesn't want to open up to me. I only know small amounts because he only speaks about it when something similar happens in the news or in life. It seems it is hard for him to open up. Not only that, we have a hard and difficult relationship. Still, these are the stories I remember...

At the age of 5, Gerardo Cerezo Romero lived in Zacatepec, Morelos, México. He lived with his mother Maria Dolores, his two sisters (Gabriela and Daniela), and his father. His father would go to work but, when it became Friday, he would not show up until late at night. He would waste all his money to get drunk. His mother sometimes didn't have enough money to buy food. So, she would feed them tortillas with beans. Gerardo would get his tortilla as a taco and leave the table. He would walk to his neighbor`s house (back then it was like a ranch) where there was a cow. The cow knew him, so she would not hurt him at all. He would lie down and drink milk while he bit his taco. Then, he fell asleep with half of his taco still in his hand. His mother knew where to find him; she didn't panic when he didn't come home early. She would pick him up and take him home.

When he was nine years old, Gerardo decided to leave his mom and his two sisters. This happened after his dad left them, and Gerardo decided to help out his mother. He left for the U.S. "Para el sueño Americano." He only got to Tijuana, where he stayed with friends he met on the way. He found a job washing cars to pay for "el coyote" to pass him to the other side of Tijuana. He also saved money to send to his mother, Maria Dolores, to buy medication for herself. She had cancer and tried everything to stay alive for her two daughters and Gerardo. After a couple of months, he received a call that his mother had gotten worse, so he had to go back home. After several months at home, his mother passed way and he had to work full time to help out his sisters.

When he was in his late 20s or early 30s, he worked for a man who handled money for the "Consular", someone who loaned money to people. Gerardo helped him as much as possible to get money from the cabinet to the people who asked for it. While on break, people always questioned him why he never took money from the cabin, which was like a safe-deposit box. The cabin held all the money that the "Consular" brought in. This money was to help people in need pay their bills. It then had to be repaid back to the "Consular." It ran almost like a bank, the difference being that it helped pay for the people's lands. Gerardo never thought about taking money, until one day he saw all the money and said, "I could easily get a bill from the center and he would not notice." He realized at that moment that if he did this he would become a thief, and would go on to lose his friends and other people's trust.

Even though these are small memories, I manage to get a glimpse into my dad's past. They might not be big memories, but small things do count. I hope that one day he opens up to me and tells me about his life, before it is too late and we go in different directions. It makes me sad to notice that we don't have a great relationship. Life has been hard for him as a single parent, taking care of me, my sisters, and my brother. Now each of us is going our separate ways. I hope that he can open up and not leave me wondering who he was and is.

A Discovered Talent

OMAR CRUZ

Roberto Cruz

A young man named Roberto Cruz from a small rural town in Jalisco faced struggles, lack of resources, and much painful treatment by his peers.

As time passed, Roberto's family suffered from poverty. Many of his brothers and sisters couldn't finish middle school because they had to work and provide for his family. He made up his mind to come up with a solution to all his family problems. This was "The American Dream". He had family living in the United States. He knew that they would help him get a job once he got to the United States.

Being a food vendor was his only option due to the fact that he didn't have any experience in any other jobs. Roberto struggled, and walking eight hours a day was very tiring for him. His legs hurt every day and he got many blisters. They were like getting cut by a blade. After struggling but getting nowhere with this job, he decided to go in search of less tiring work. A furniture factory caught his eye. This job was like heaven. It was less demanding, but sadly he lost it. The owner of the factory couldn't handle the business and had no choice but to sell the company. The new owner fired all the workers who didn't have legal papers. Roberto was one of the affected workers.

Roberto kept searching for a new job but he couldn't find one. Days later, he found out that his brother-in-law played in a mariachi band. His brother-in-law talked to him about how this job worked and how much each band player earned. Roberto was very interested and glad he found a job, so he quickly found a teacher and learned to play an instrument. The teacher was very strict. Roberto began to hate him because every time he played a note incorrectly, he would get hit with a stick on his hand. As years passed, he got good at it and mastered all the notes so he could play them without making any mistakes. He found a new talent and became a good mariachi player. Now he gives thanks to the strictness of his teacher. He learned how to play an instrument, something he never thought he would be able to do. His life changed after all his struggles, but to him it was worth it. Now he is able to sustain his family financially and his job isn't as tiring as the ones he had before.

After all the struggles, the lack of resources, and mistreatments he suffered, he was able to discover a talent he never knew he had. It took courage to be a strong person and to not let anything get in his way. He discovered what he really had inside, and found success.

Negative To Positive

MICHELLE DURAN

Drugs, weapons, and violence were what David had grown up with. He joined a gang at the age of twelve and lived in constant danger of getting killed. He smoked weed, skipped school, and drank beer. His siblings Eric, Fernie, Tito, Gonzalo, and Letty were also involved in a gang, and often got into trouble.

Eric's Grave

They feared no consequences. It wasn't like David woke up one day and said, "This is the day I'll destroy my life." As a young child, he was raised well with great loving parents who went to Assumption Church every Sunday. He was a decent kid, but one day he made a decision that forever changed not only his life but the life of his family as well.

The day his brother Eric passed away was New Year's Eve. David woke up feeling like something wasn't right. What was bugging him? David made a phone call to Mexico to talk to his mother, Delia. They wished each other a "Feliz Año Nuevo" and Delia suddenly began to cry, "Como me gustaría estar con ustedes para celebrar el año nuevo. Dile a todos que los amo mucho."

"Si mama, no se preocupe. Te amo," said David.

~

After talking to his mother, David felt better and went to do his errands. He went grocery shopping for New Year's Eve dinner, and got his kids ready for the celebration. He took a warm shower, put on new clothes, and combed his hair. They left to his sister Letty's house, where they celebrated the New Year. When they got to Letty's house, everyone was waiting for them and began to eat.

At ten o'clock at night, David's phone rang. It was David's friend Ernesto calling him to say that something horrible had happened to Eric. David was in shock, he didn't move. Ernesto didn't hesitate to tell him that Eric got shot in the chest and was at the hospital in really bad condition. He didn't know what to do or think. Right away, David and his family went to the hospital, but didn't have to wait that long to hear the bad news from the doctor. Eric didn't make it.

Everyone but David was crying hysterically. He showed no emotions. He couldn't believe it. When he got to his house he felt a rush of emotions running through him. David felt confused, scared, and lonely. Then, he felt angry with the world. He cursed, punched the wall, and broke things. In that very moment, all he wanted was revenge. David went to his room and pulled out a box from the closet where he kept his gun. He unlocked the box and stared at the gun for a while. He put the gun inside his pocket and left to his friend Ernesto's house.

The gang gathered at Ernesto's house. They were planning on how to get revenge. David thought about Eric's kids. He knew the pain and suffering they were going through. He knew how it felt to lose someone because he had lost many of his friends. He didn't want his kids to go through the same situation. David knew he couldn't risk anything and make a mistake because he had a family to take care of. He left Ernesto's house to go with his family.

Innocence

LESLIE ESCOBEDO

Adelina Romero, an eighteen year old, was playing with her brother in the front yard. Because her little brother Erick loved flying kites, Adelina took time to play with him. In fact, she taught him how to fly kites.

On a sunny Sunday, Adelina's brother-in-law Eugenio hurriedly parked his car in the street. He made so much noise that the chickens outside of the house ran into the house immediately. All that noise scared Erick. He let his kite fall down and ran to hide behind Adelina. She thought her brother-in-law was drunk because of the huge fight he had with his wife, Adelina's sister. She asked, "What's wrong?"

He answered, "Nothing. I just need you to come with me."

Adelina told him she couldn't leave Erick alone. Also, he was getting so anxious that she didn't want to go with him. Adelina asked him if she could take Erick with them. He said no.

Suddenly, he grabbed her by the arm and forced her in the car. Erick watched fearfully. He cried really loudly. She tried to get out of the car but he locked the doors.

She told Erick to go tell somebody what was happening and to ask for help, but he didn't understand her. He just stayed in front of the house motionless. Once Eugenio got in the car, she asked him to let her out, but he started to freak out. He was nervous, but he said everything was going to be alright if she stayed quiet.

He started the car, pulled out of the driveway, and drove to the main road. She thought he was kidnapping her. It was stupid to think that about her brother-in-law. It couldn't be possible. They were family. So she just tried to relax and let him talk. He told her he couldn't say where he was taking her because she was too young to understand. They stayed silent for a while. Then she asked him questions, but he didn't answer. She begged him to tell her everything and promised she would not say anything. She even said she would help him, but inside she was really scared. She thought he was going to hit her. Soon, exhausted and tired, she fell asleep. She woke up thinking she had just had a nightmare, but she soon started crying when she realized she wasn't having a nightmare. This was cruel reality. She didn't know how many hours she slept, but the moment she opened her eyes, she started to feel something she couldn't quite understand. Adelina wanted to escape from the car, but she knew it was dangerous. Instead she tried to let the feeling of being scared disappear. She was just about to ask questions, but he said, "Don't start asking questions, because I won't answer you!"

They drove for a while in silence. She was still very frightened and he was still nervous. She realized this because of the way he was driving. She asked if she could turn on the radio. He said it was fine as long she didn't sing. She thought that if she was about to be killed or raped, or if something else bad was about to happen to her, she might as well enjoy one last song, a song she would hear for the last time in her life. She thought it was stupid to think this, but she couldn't get rid of that thought.

Eugenio finally started to talk. He told her that a friend of his wanted to meet her and that was where they were going. They were going to a placed called Tulancingo.

Adelina asked him why somebody would want to meet her, and who he was.

Eugenio told her he would tell her if she promised she would help him. She agreed.

Eugenio explain that he owed money to that guy, and he was

asking for the money, but Eugenio didn't have enough to pay him back. So, the guy explained that he liked Adelina and would forget about the debt if he took Adelina to his house and introduced her to him. Eugenio had thought about it and agreed that he would take her to his house.

Adelina was shocked and relieved at the same time. She asked what she had to do exactly. Eugenio told her that she had to go inside the house to meet the guy, chat with him, and be nice. Confused, she asked how old he was. He was twenty-five. Then she asked if he was cute. He told her he was kind of cute. Adelina thought about it and asked Eugenio for a favor in return for the one she was doing for him. She wanted to drive on the way back home. Eugenio said yes.

She entered the house and introduced herself to the guy. They sat on the couch and he offered her something to drink. They talked casually, then he moved closer to her and grabbed her hand. She refused his advances, but he didn't pay attention. He tried to kiss her and started touching her. She immediately got up and told him to stop. He yelled at her, saying that she knew what she was doing and that she had to do it or else Eugenio could go to jail and that would affect her sister. Adelina started to cry and told him to let her go, that they would find a way to pay him. But he didn't listen.

A Teenage Pregnancy

AGUSTIN ESPARZA

Eva's the oldest of seven children. She's responsible for everything at home. She does the cooking, cleaning, gets her younger brothers and sister ready for school each and every morning, and works a part-time job at a taco stand. Eva's parents never showed love and affection; they weren't the ones who worried when something went wrong with the young ones.

Eva and her family

Eva had just found out about her pregnancy. She felt happy about being pregnant, but not about the relationship she was in. He wasn't the best boyfriend. He often physically and mentally abused her, but the only thing that ran through her head was her parents.

When the news of her pregnancy got to her father he immediately demanded that she have an abortion. He found out how much it cost and said he was willing to pay for it. So many emotions ran through her head; those words tore her heart into a million pieces. She felt confused. She didn't know what to do. She already knew that having an abortion was against both her family's religion and her gut feelings. Yet, she felt ready to get rid of her abusive boyfriend and had just gotten accepted to attend college. Eva decided to keep her baby, but her pregnancy wasn't easy. It was difficult in every possible way -- mentally, emotionally, and physically. The only reason she kept her head up was for her baby. Hearing her baby's heart beat and feeling the kicks gave her a reason to keep going. She went on with her life and tried to succeed in making her parents believe in her, but every day they made it clear to her that they were disappointed and embarrassed by the choices she had made. Her mother told her not to show her stomach or wear cute maternity clothes because being pregnant was nothing to be proud of at a young age. Eva's father didn't exchange a word with her during her pregnancy. Eva felt confused and lonely. She had also lost many of her friends. Many of her friends' mothers asked not to speak to her because it was an embarrassment. During one of her doctor's appointments, he told her, "Your blood pressure is rising. I am afraid you could have a stroke and that your baby's heart might stop beating." Eva went home, packed her baby's clothes and told her mother the big day was here.

Eva asked her mother to advise her through the delivery. Her mother told her, "Sorry, but I have a job to attend to. Once you have your baby you'll know what life's about." Eva had to no choice but to go by herself. By the time she got to the hospital things became worse; her baby's heart was beating slowly.

The doctors ordered an emergency C-section. Everyone was rushing around. She was trying to think straight and not panic. After a couple of hours her son was born. Eva was in shock over how fast it happened. After giving birth, she had surgery and wasn't able to hold her son due to her high fever. Two days later. Eva got the chance to hold her son. Then Eva realized she just had a baby and that there was nothing in the world that could take that away from her. Eva felt happy to see that her baby's eyes were full of love every time he looked at her.

Six weeks later, Eva returned to school and joined the drill team. Eva started doing different hairstyles for different occasions, and charged her customers five dollars. Soon, Eva got an offer to babysit during the night. With that little money, Eva was able to afford to buy her baby diapers, clothes, and other necessary items. Eva chose to breast feed because it was healthier for her son and it helped out financially.

Everything was really hard for her to accomplish by herself, but there was no going back. Eva kept her head up and didn't let anything get in her way. Eva graduated from high school, and always came in the top three in her drill team competitions. This journey in her life was definitely the hardest obstacle she's had to overcome, but she has never been happier, with her son full of love and joy.

One Special Dance

DENISE FELIX

Sole

My grandpa told my mom she was going to get an opportunity to dance with Celia Cruz on stage. My mom smiled enthusiastically. Her eyes filled with excitement. Full of happiness, she hugged her father. She went home to tell her mom the good news. Her mom gave her the money to go buy a dress. She couldn't believe that this was going to happen. She filled up with joy. She knew this would be a day she would never forget, and that this was the greatest experience that had happened to her so far.

She needed an elegant dress, so she asked her mom to buy her one as soon as she got home. She went to Goodwill, a place where they sell used clothes. When she got there, she searched for the perfect dress. She found a burgundy and black one. The front was short, up to the knees, while in the back it had a long tail. The top was made of shiny black lace with sparkles on it. It tied in the back of the neck and the zipper was also in the back. It had sequins that shined when light hit them.

Her hair was pulled back in a bun of curls. It was held up by a handful of bobby pins. Two strands of hair pulled out, curling down the side of her face. She wore just enough make-up to look beautiful, yet natural. She put some blush on her pink cheeks and put on some burgundy lipstick. She wore black, four-inch high heels. She liked what she was wearing. She felt special for the night and just kept smiling the whole time.

As soon as she was ready, she and her father left for the theatre in Chinatown. The decorations were extraordinary! Flowers hung from the ceiling. The mellow lights shined on the people who showed up to the concert. People arrived in elegant clothes, the women in evening gowns and the guys in tuxedos. Some even arrived in limousines or nice fancy cars. A lot of people showed up for this event. My mom went backstage to talk to Celia Cruz to find out how she was going to go up on stage. When the show started, my mom went to sit in the front row with the audience and watched the show. Celia Cruz wore a shiny, one-sleeve dress. The dress was pearl white with sequins, which shone brightly so people could spot it from a distance. After she finished a couple of songs, she took a rest and the audience applauded. When she went back out, Celia Cruz announced she was going to call one of her biggest fans from the audience, and looked at my mom.

The lights pointed at my mom and Celia Cruz announced that Sole was going to go up on stage and dance with her. Celia Cruz reached out for my mom's hand. She was so excited, and also a bit nervous because she didn't want to mess up in front of a lot of people. The people didn't know this was going to happen; it was a last minute thing. They danced while Celia Cruz sang one of her famous songs, titled "El Carnival." The audience clapped while they danced. As soon as they finished, Celia Cruz hugged my mom and bowed down. The crowd was amazed at what a great job she had done dancing with Celia Cruz. They liked what Celia Cruz did, and everyone knew her as someone who liked to make others happy. My mom got off stage with tears of happiness. She couldn't believe that she had just danced with her idol. This was a day she would never forget: the happiest moment of her life.

An Unforgettable Day

MICHAEL FERNANDEZ

June 26, 1972 was a day he would remember. For him, it started as a typical Sunday morning at the Harbor UCLA Medical Center in Torrance, California. As he walked in, he could smell the scent of coffee and donuts drifting in the air. Jose Fernandez had barely checked in for work at the hospital at 6:00 a.m., and his wife at the time, Beatriz Fernandez, had been having contractions since 3:00 a.m. His emotions had him anxious all day, but he had to maintain his focus while working with the x-ray machine. His day seemed to lag as he checked the equipment and took glimpses at the clock, hoping it was time for his shift to end. He had been taking shifts with his friends, running up and down to check to see if his daughter had been born yet. The day seemed to lag even more as he glimpsed the clock. It seemed as if time was toying with him, making every minute as slow as it could possibly get.

The x-ray machine was prepared and cleaned for the quick screenings of patients with all kinds of broken body parts. Still, while he was helping and working, he could not help but wonder if she was coming yet or not? As the morning passed by in the hospital, he waited to hear if his newborn baby girl was coming. It was close to 7:00 a.m. when Beatriz went into labor. He started to get nervous, so nervous that sweat beads trickled down his forehead, as if sliding down on a piece of glass, making his eyes burn.

It was June 26, 1972 when his daughter was born. He rushed to see her minutes later. The way he felt at that moment was beyond amazing; he was so happy. He felt a mix of emotions as he held her in his arms for the first time.

"*Estaba guerita,*" he said when she was born, "*y con pelo bien rubio.*"

She was the most beautiful being he had ever seen or held, he thought, and wished that those moments could last forever.

Years later, he reminisces and chuckles while saying, "*No mas me miraba con sus ojos grandes,*" and acts as if he was there. That is when your mom and I gave her the name Natalie. "*Pero cuando empezó a llorar, le dije que niñas bonitas no se lloran.*"

He loved the sound and thought of being a father, something he would not trade for the world. That feeling brought out his true being as a loving and caring father. About an hour after she was born, he headed back down to work and everyone congratulated him.

He was so happy and excited that he had almost forgotten how to control the x-rays. The first thing he did was find a place to stay and start his new family. They lived in an apartment, but he was starting to make good money. He decided the best thing to do was to give his family what he never had. So he went off and found a huge house, at least for those days, in the city of Riverside. There, he started his family and provided for them. He did what he could for his family, and for him, at the end of the day, it was all worth it.

Born To A Big Change

EDGAR GARCIA

The pain was unbearable. In her stomach, she felt the baby already wanting to come out. She heard the doctors talking, so she closed her eyes for a second. Her memories began to flood her mind.

She remembered living in a three-story apartment, on the third floor. At that time, she dated a man who later on became my younger brother's dad. Since she started to feel a connection to him, she decided to move in with him. They moved into his big house. Because he also had part of his family living with them, it felt awkward at the start. Soon, they got comfortable with each other.

That changed. One day they decided that they would just stop talking to her. She noticed they started acting strange, like they didn't even know her. They started looking for problems with her. She tried to avoid them and to just ignore them to prevent any problems from arising between her boyfriend and her. His family just kept on looking for any little excuse to start a problem. She had had enough, so they decided to leave that house immediately.

She woke up and the doctors informed her that they needed to perform a C-section.

She stared at the colorless surroundings and started thinking about all the problems—moving back to the apartments, and being visited by my brother's father, whose attitude had changed drastically. She remembered waiting for Estevan, my brother's dad, a couple of times. Sometimes he showed up; sometimes he forgot. When he did show up, he took her into the bathroom and argued with her. She never knew what would happen to her when he showed up. Everyone else just sat on the sofa and watched TV. After they finished in the bathroom, he walked out and headed straight to the door without saying a word. She stayed in the bathroom and sobbed, trying to hide her tears from her family.

She had a friend at her old job. Her friend had told her about moving to Oregon, a very different place from California. She thought nothing of it, but soon she got tired of how that man and his family treated her. One day she decided that she and her son would accompany her friend on his permanent trip to Oregon, thinking it would be a great way to forget what was going on with her family. She drove to the airport and off they went to their new home, Oregon.

It was not her first time on an airplane. When she got to Oregon, she entered a casino with her son. It did not take long for one of the security guards to notice her child, so they were immediately told to step out and leave the casino.

The season was winter. It was very cold, and she had never seen snow before. She remembered that her son was so excited to see the snow for the first time. She needed to find a decent job in order to take care of her family, but there were none available. Luckily, she found a job opening at a store, and the manager gave it to her. Although being surrounded by snow was exciting at the start, she got tired of the weather. She was not used to such cold temperatures. She gained weight, and realized that she was pregnant. Due to her pregnancy and the cold weather, she decided to leave Oregon and move back to California. She found an apartment, far away from my little brother's dad. A couple of months later, she gave birth to my little brother Steven.

Family Man

ISABEL GARCIA

On the quiet morning of June 1, 1953 in Durango, Maria and Carlos Garcia were expecting their first born son, Jose Garcia. Soon after the birth, the family portrait faded away. Carlos stepped out of the picture. Having no father to keep the family together, my dad's life became a struggle. Once my dad came to an understanding age, he had to become the "man of the house," working his whole life, giving up his dreams to give hope to others.

The only boy, my dad was the jewel of the family, playing pranks and running around. The sound of laughter and toys filled the Garcia home. When it was time, my dad entered elementary school in his hometown of Ignacio Ramirez. At the age of ten, his mother broke the news to him that they were moving to Torreon, where his older sister and her husband lived. Making the best of it, Jose got a job in town and made new friends while going to school. By the time he was thirteen, he returned home. His dream of being a school teacher and furthering his education came to a halt. The dilemma of the financial burden came as a reality for the young man. My father started working in the fields and soon the fresh open space, tractors, and the birds up above became my father's life for four years, from the ages of fourteen to eighteen. His main priority was keeping his family together and providing a home and food.

The lost teen years and the pressure of maintaining a family was so much for him that he became rebellious, drinking and staying out late, getting into problems with the law. My dad was losing control. At the age of eighteen, my dad went into the military, and the discipline he learned and endured made him the strict man he is today.

In 1973, once he was out of the military, my dad sat his mother and little sister down in their home and told them, "I have decided that staying here has no future." A few weeks later all three packed and came to the United States. They left the home where they had grown up, and all the memories stayed behind in the home. A new life was awaiting. To my dad's surprise, the American dream was a make believe story. Trying to provide for his family, he got a job as a forklift driver. For ten years he kept that job. With a home and a steady paycheck, life seemed to become much easier.

In 1982, my father married my mother. Happily, their new family started, to everyone's joy, with a boy, Servando Garcia! My father's eyes glittered so happily at his new family. But the happiness soon disappeared as he lost his job.

"How can this happen," he kept thinking. Where would he turn? Sadly, he turned to alcohol as a solution, and he quietly started his downfall.

A few years later, a man came to him and offered him a job as a housing manager. From there on, his future turned bright, or so it seemed, with three kids of his own and a wife. Still by his side were his mom and little sister. The stress was killing him inside, though, with no one knowing my dad was still struggling with his alcohol addiction. This addiction reached the point where his body gave up on him. A quiet normal dinner came to a devastating end when my father collapsed. Rushed to the hospital, the doctors told him one more drop of alcohol would kill him. Since that day, he has known this was not a life he wanted for his children. He wanted to be there to see his kids live their dreams and achieve anything they wanted and beyond.

Jose Garcia was born the man of the house and to this day no one can take that title from him. Through every struggle he grew into a stronger person. Every step he took was to become a better man and now, at the age of 57, he can look back and be proud to say he never let his family down.

Building Success

STEPHANIE GONZALES

Palms sweating and heart pounding, a young seventeen year old scrawny looking Robie Aguila did not know whether or not he would get the job. After applying for many jobs, Robie hoped and prayed that he would at least get one. Sitting, waiting nervously at home for a call, the phone finally rang. Listening, fearing the thought of bad news, Robie heard differently. With great excitement over the big news of getting hired at a Boys and Girls Club, Robie thought to himself, "Wow, I got it and this is it, time to step it up and be a man not only for me but for my family as well."

Robie quickly sprinted to his mother's job to tell her the great news. Catching his breath, Robie tried explaining to his mom that by his working, she could quit one of her two jobs. She gave him a confused look. Robie knew his mother couldn't believe the news, and knew she wouldn't quit any of her jobs. This made Robie very anxious about working. He hoped that once he started his job and started showing his mom that he could provide for her, she would know that she would be in good hands.

On his way home, Robie knew he had to make one last stop. He entered the front door of his grandfather's house knowing that he would need to get advice from the man who's been there from the start and was the greatest "father" anyone could ever have. Listening to what his "father" had to say, he understood that being a man would take strength, responsibility, and determination. With that knowledge, Robie knew that no matter how small his part at his new job, he could achieve and become something bigger.

By getting a job, Robie knew that not only would he help support his family, but that he could turn this chance into a huge opportunity. After a week of anxious waiting, the big day finally arrived. Being only seventeen, he knew they would start him off as a staff member. As he walked through the building, mentored by his boss, he saw all the children and teens his own age having fun and participating in the activities they had going on there. Seeing that, Robie assumed his job as a staff member would be easy and all he would have to do was play with the kids. After a month, Robie definitely changed his views about everything.

After almost a year, balancing school and a job, Robie wanted to give up and quit. He went home and told his mother he didn't want to work anymore, that he was tired of being the teen with no social life. Robie saw how his mother reacted and heard the solution she had for him. She would get her old job back or find a new one. At that point, Robie thought about the past and how exhausted his mother looked when she came home, and how she stressed when it came time to pay the bills. Robie thought real hard about coming all this way, working hard, helping to provide for his mother, and almost getting to where he could move up and become a secretary. Robie knew he couldn't give up now.

Robie needed a bit more of a push to keep himself from quitting. He thought about the secretary job his boss had offered him the previous month. Knowing that it would be difficult and that he would have to work even harder, Robie also considered the much better pay. Regretting his early decision to reject it, Robie felt nervous about asking his boss if the job was still available. But Robie believed that if his boss hadn't seen the potential in him, she wouldn't have offered the job in the first place. This gave Robie the confidence to take the initiative and go ask for the job. Walking toward his boss's office, Robie thought long and hard about what to say. When he stepped inside her office, he began asking about the promotion she offered him not long ago. Robie was amazed that his boss was actually hoping he would change his mind. Working in his own office and dealing with paperwork at the age of nineteen, Robie felt the responsibility that a man should have. Robie knew all of his hard work had finally paid off.

After working for a month in his new office, Robie came across blueprints of the club and underneath it a new design. Interested in this, he went to his boss and began asking questions. He learned about the new ideas for the club. Robie knew he had to stick around and be part of this new project in some way: a new adventure for young Robie Aguila.

Maternal Love

MIGUEL HERNANDEZ

A cold morning, on March 17, the wind was hitting an old house where a family reunion was taking place. Delfina Ruiz, a strong woman who always smiled, reflected a face full of seriousness. She gathered all her family members to say "adios" to them. Many marvelous stories of a country full of hope floated in her mind. She decided to travel to the United States of America because of all the stories she had heard about families living in houses with beautiful gardens and owning a convertible Mercedes Benz. With all those stories floating in her mind, she gave her three little children the warmest hug she had ever given. Her warm hug could easily have melted the North Pole with its maternal heat. Anahy, her only daughter of seven years, knew that her mom planned to emigrate to a different country and that the journey was dangerous. She looked into her mom's eyes and with an affectionate voice said, "Mama, cuidate y no nos olvides." The other two kids, Hugo and Irving, were younger and did not realize that mom planned to leave them with their grandma.

Delfina remembers sitting on a white bus with green stripes around it and huge letters that said "Mexico-Tijuana." She spent not more than one week in the city of Tijuana, Baja California, Mexico before crossing the border on a cold night.

The coyotes put a ladder against a rusty fence to help her jump it easily. She jumped the rusty fence and ran to a McDonald's closest to the border. She entered the McDonald's and pretended to be confident in the environment, but her legs shook the whole time she stayed in the famous restaurant. Fortunately, the coyote did not take long and went to pick her up in a green SUV. The coyote took her and four other illegal immigrants, some of whom were dropped off in San Diego.

The three hours from Tijuana to Los Angeles were an eternity for her. She pictured her three children playing around in the old house she left behind. Once she got to the United States all she desired was to call her children in Mexico. She looked for a public telephone and communicated with her children. Delfina wanted to cry and smile at the same time when she heard Anahy's, Hugo's, and Irving's voices. Her heart pounded like never before. She felt herself grow warm in her heart and soul at that moment.

Tears rolled down her cheeks when her children asked, "When are you coming back?" She froze and didn't answer their question because she did not know the answer.

During the six months she lived separated from her children, she worked in a clothes factory. Frequently, she ended up with tears rolling down her cheeks. Her tears were filled with dreams: dreams about returning to Mexico, her home country, and of seeing her children. Delfina could not live without her children for more than six months and decided to go back. She stills remembers the day she bought the ticket to fly back to her country. While she boarded the airplane her mind reflected about her decision to leave her children behind. Relieved that nothing happened to her children during her absence, she thanked God for protecting them while she was gone. She was glad because if something had happened to them, she would have become insane. She will never forget Anahy's, Hugo's, and Irving's faces when they saw her arrive in Mexico City. The three of them screamed "Mama" at the same time. They wanted to cry, but they were embarrassed to do so in public.

Delfina ran towards them and gave them an enormous hug. She wanted them to forgive her, but she felt only a sensation in her throat and no words came out. So she gave them a hug instead.

The Loss Of A Child

JUSTO JUAREZ

Fabiola Juarez had a beautiful life. She married Jose Juarez and within two years they had one beautiful child and expected another. Fabiola's pregnancy became an ecstatic and wonderful experience until a life changing tragedy occurred. Fabiola had barely reached the third trimester when she fell. That changed her life as well as that of the baby she had inside her.

On the evening of April 23, Fabiola went downstairs. As the stairs had proven to be a difficult challenge, she held her stomach as she took each step. She made it down the last step, filled with relief, and headed towards another room when she stepped on a puddle and fell. The slippery floor and the sandals she was wearing made her fall in a way that caused her legs to spread apart and her stomach to almost touch the floor. After this happened, she started looking around for help. Once she realized no one was around to help her, she managed to get up on her own. She soon became very frightened and quickly headed towards her bed. The fear in her head made her stay in bed for the rest of the day. Around 7:00 p.m., her husband came home, and she told him that she had slipped on a puddle and fell down. During the night, her stomach started hurting a lot and she noticed something was wrong because her stomach seemed to be rough.

Fabiola told Jose that she couldn't feel the baby move, so they immediately went to the hospital. Once they got to the hospital, the doctor examined her, and when he finished he told her that he couldn't hear the baby's heart, and that she had to urgently go to another hospital. They then took her to another hospital in an ambulance. When she got there, they performed an ultrasound and told her that her baby had died. A while later, they injected a medicine into her so that the baby could come out even though it was dead.

Her entire life became depressing. The next day she left the hospital and she saw other women leaving with their babies in their arms, very grateful, while she left the hospital very heartbroken with her baby inside a wooden box. She got worse because her parents, thinking that it might affect her health, didn't let Fabiola go to the baby's funeral, .

Life will forever be difficult, and these tragic memories haunt Fabiola until this day. She has moved on from this incident, although tears do come out whenever she tells this heartbreaking story.

Crazy Situations

MICHELLE LIRA

Laying down on his bed, Michael thinks about the crazy things he has gone through in his life, from the days he can remember to today, when he's 35. In life, he made so many choices that he couldn't control, like falling in love with his sixth grade history teacher, and getting heartbroken at the end of it all...

Falling in love is something that happens all the time, from the kid in elementary to the oldest people in the world. Love, most of the time, is uncontrollable. For Michael, love was uncontrollable. His feelings were growing, getting stronger for his history teacher. She was in her mid-twenties to early thirties, thin, with light skin, long red curly hair, and blue eyes that were framed by big, pink, nerd glasses. This was the first love of his life. He always looked forward to going to school because he knew that he would see her.

The kids that knew Michael would trip out because they knew Michael as the big troublemaker, not caring what grades he got, always giving his teachers a hard time, and always going in tardy and skipping classes. But when it came to this class, he was always one of the first ones to arrive, sitting in the front seat, paying attention in class, raising his hand when he knew the answer, and regulating the students that made fun of the teacher or tried to be destructive. The kids actually listened because they were afraid of him and because they all respected Michael.

~

One day a new boy entered some of his classes. This boy was a little taller than Michael, white, and a little bit chubbier than Michael. This boy always challenged Michael. He would always cap on him, calling him "nigger" and telling him fat jokes. Michael knew that this new student would soon know not to mess with him because the other students knew Michael's ways, and would tell this white boy to be careful. But it seemed like this never happened.

Days passed and nothing seemed to change with this kid. He kept acting like he was "the shit," always trying to make Michael mad to see if what the people told him was true.

Toward the middle of the first semester, the Miss was teaching about Nigeria. The white boy said, "Hey, you fucken' black nigger, that's were you came from, huh?"

Michael just looked at him with extreme rage because he was tired of dealing with the white boy's hate.

Michael got closer to the right side of his seat, leaned closer to the white boy, and told him, "Look, you white piece of shit, you better shut the fuck up before you get your ass pummeled to the floor!"

The white boy looked at Michael and said, "Oowwww, I'm sooooo scared of the most fattest, most stupidest kid in this whole world," while lifting his hands as if he were afraid of him.

Without being aware of himself, Michael stood up and started screaming at the boy.

The white boy, feeling threatened, stood up and said, "What you fucken' fat ni......"

"Both of you guys side down!!!" yelled the history teacher.

The two responded quickly and sat down. They had never seen this side of her. She just closed her eyes and took a deep breath.

When she opened her eyes, she just told Michael, "Those words aren't nice, Michael." Shaking her head in disappointment, she added, "And nigger was a term used for lazy people, when the Africans became slaves. They used the word to describe laziness towards the Africans even though they weren't lazy at all... if anything, the white people were the lazy ones..."

She looked directly at the white boy boy with a little anger in her eyes, but at the same time told all of her students this interesting fact of hers.

"And you, young man, should study more and pay more attention in class instead of making smart remarks in this class..."

That day Michael had butterflies in his stomach thinking about how the Miss had defended him in class, thinking that the Miss loved him just as much as he loved her.

"I still have time to catch up to her. She's only, like, twenty-five. I could catch up to her in a couple of years... I could do this and we're going to live happily ever after..."

From that day on, he would imagine the day when they would get married. Days, then weeks, passed and there was only less than a month left of school, and then everyone would go on vacation. It was a Monday.

The Miss looked extremely happy and Michael thought she looked even more beautiful than the other days.

"Class," she told the students. "I'm only going to be here for two more weeks because I'm going on vacation early," she said with a smile on her face.

Maggie, one of the shortest girls in class, asked why. The Miss looked at her with an expression on her face as if she had been asked a life-or-death question.

"Well, I'm going to get married with my boyfriend that I have been with since college..."

Michael's mouth dropped, and his little heart broke into millions of pieces. The Miss kept talking because Maggie wanted to know more. But Michael's mind trailed off.

"What happened to what we had? I thought we had something strong... how could this happen?"

Michael felt depressed. Every time he saw her, the more his heart would break.

Then he started thinking, "Well, maybe the marriage won't last long. Maybe they will get divorced and then I will have my chance with her, and by then I will be old enough to get married with her."

That made him feel better. Although he knew that she was getting married, he still had a slight spark of hope in him. The last day she was at school before she went on her early vacation, she took the boyfriend to school to show him off to the class.

The first thought that jumped into Michael's mind was, "Damn, this guy looks so cool. Thank God this is going to be our sub for the rest of the month. I'd like to look like him when I'm older -- tall and buff."

Then the Miss came in. Michael was looking at the way that guy was staring at her, and he didn't like it. Then, when the bell rang she closed the door so that nothing would interrupt the class.

She looked at the man and smiled. "Class," she said, while looking at the man and holding out her hand. "This is my husband."

She was so happy, and then she told her husband, "This is the best class in the world!"

Michael's jaw dropped again and then he just put his head down on the table.

"Damn, he's even better than I thought. I even looked up to him! I am so out of luck. How could this have happened!?"

"Michael," the Miss asked Michael with a whisper. "Are you okay?"

Michael just looked at her, trying to not let his true feelings show.

"My head hurts a lot, that's all," he said.

The Miss just looked at him with worried eyes. Michael put his head down, knowing that he would tear up if he kept looking into her eyes.

Then she asked, "Would you like to go to the nurse and call your parents to go home?"

All Michael could say was "yes." She moved to her desk and all he could hear were her heels and the movie playing.

"Come and get your note, Michael," she said.

Michael got his stuff together, picked up the note from her desk, and left.

While he was walking out of the class, he heard her say, "See you next semester, Michael!" Her voice faded as the door shut.

The door closed completely. He didn't look back and started to run. Now he knew that he really didn't have a chance at all.

Journey To America

NANCY LOPEZ

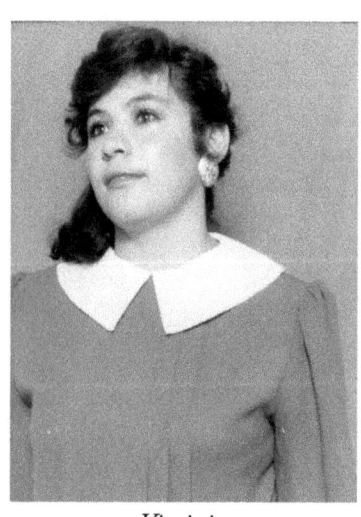

Virginia

My mom, Virginia, is one of seven children that my grandmother Alejandra had. Their dad died when they were all young; therefore, they helped their mother financially. As they got older, one of the older daughters, Vita, decided to come to California in search of a job to help out the family and bring them with her to have a better life. At the age of twenty-five, she had enough money to bring her mom and her uncle Mario to Los Angeles with her, so that they could work and bring the rest of the family. This is how my mom's journey to Los Angeles began.

The cold dark night before leaving Chihuahua, Mexico in 1976, my mom felt gloomy as she went to say good-bye to some family members. That night, when the strong storm of hail and wind started, the moon was full as she confessed to her mother that she didn't want to go to Los Angeles and leave her behind. They called her sister Vita so she could help ease my mom's soreness. However, that wasn't enough to get her a good night's sleep. She slept, thinking of what her future in Los Angeles was going to be like.

At four in the morning the next day, my mom got ready to leave along with my uncle Mario and his wife Maria. Without eating, they left the house in the cold to board the plane to Parral. My grandmother had cooked breakfast for them, but they were in such a hurry to leave because they didn't want to miss the plane, that the food was left on the table. The flight took one hour. When they landed, they were freezing and starving, so they went to one of their cousin's house to get something to eat and spend the night.

The next day they took the bus to Tijuana. It was a 24-hour ride. They spent three days in Tijuana in a hotel. The first day they arrived in Tijuana they didn't eat anything because they didn't have a lot of money. The second day they just ate snacks. By the third day they were super hungry, so they finally bought something to eat for all three. Then they got the call from the lady that was going to help them get across the border. On the fourth day, they went to her house in the afternoon. Another guy picked them up that night and took them to the border.

He left them waiting at the border for a few hours because he had to go get other people who were going to cross as well. While waiting there, they saw other people selling food and clothes. While going to buy food, my mom's sandal ripped so they decided to buy some sandals instead of eating, because she couldn't go on without shoes. Once the guy got there, he took all of them into the cold and dark mountains. They all walked with him for about two hours before he traded them off to another guy.

The second guy divided them into groups, but for some reason he left my mom behind and alone hiding under bushes so she wouldn't be seen. At this point my mom was scared because no one knew where she was and she couldn't see anything. Finally, one of the guys she meet at the border saw her, and his son helped her get out from under the bush. They told her she would be safer if she went with them, because they would help her find her brother Mario. Even though she was scared to go with them, she thought that this would be safer than waiting there to see what was next. They finally found her brother and the whole group walked together through the cold, dark mountains until they were traded off to a third guy in the middle of nowhere.

This guy didn't separate any of them but he told them that he wasn't going to stop for anyone; if anyone stopped they were going to be left behind. He gave them instructions: if they saw a helicopter or heard motorcycles or horses anywhere around them, they had to hide under bushes and trees. When my mom heard a motorcycle she quickly moved to the side to duck under some bushes, but she accidently got too close to a cactus and got stabbed in the leg. She was so scared at the moment that didn't even feel it until moments later, and her brother pulled the thorn out from her leg. They had to run to catch up to the rest of the group. They walked until five in the morning.

After that long and cold night of walking for fifteen hours, they crossed a street and ended up in San Clemente. The guy took them into a small house that had fifty people in a single room. They were all hungry and hot but couldn't leave. Thirty-five of them finally left when a trailer that was half full of bikes and furniture arrived. They loaded the people up behind the furniture. They were inside the hot, stuffy trailer for six hours. Once they got to Los Angeles, everyone was pulled out and some of them fainted because of the limited air and excessive heat inside the trailer.

My mom, uncle, and his wife waited an hour for a van to pick them up and take them to Lorena Street, where their sister Vita was going to go pick them up and give the guy the money. After giving him the money, he let them go and they hugged Vita before getting into her car and driving away. Finally, after being on her journey for seven days, she was reunited with her sister and quickly called her mother in Mexico to let her know that she got to Los Angeles safely.

A Pregnant Story

NICHOLAS MANRIQUEZ

In the month of June, Sabrina found out that motherhood would come at the age of seventeen, just as she was finishing up her junior year. Sabrina and her friend Mira went to Planned Parenthood to take the pregnancy test. Sabrina did not want to hear the news from the doctor saying she was pregnant. The first thing that ran through Sabrina's mind was what she was going to do now. Was she going to keep the baby or not? Would she tell her mother? At her age, Sabrina didn't feel ready to become a mother. Who does at that very young age? She could barely take care of herself.

Sabrina with Melanie

Walking home from Planned Parenthood, Sabrina had to think of how not to have the baby. Sabrina didn't plan on telling her mom the news. She felt nervous, scared, and worried. The next day at school, Sabrina needed someone to talk to about her situation, but didn't know who she should talk to. Later that day, while Sabrina and her mother Gracie were in the living room watching TV, Gracie asked Sabrina if she was pregnant.

Sabrina answered, "NO!" Gracie knew something wasn't right,

because she had a motherly instinct. Later in the week, in the same room, doing the same thing, Gracie asked her again if she was pregnant. Sabrina took a while to reply and said yes. Her mom asked what she was planning on doing. Sabrina replied that she didn't know. In July, Sabrina decided to keep the baby because she was already three months pregnant. When she told her friends about being pregnant, the first thing her friends said was that they hoped Sabrina was going to have a girl! From there, Sabrina decided to tell her brother. She was nervous to tell him, since she didn't know what he would say or think.

The time had arrived, and Sabrina placed herself in the kitchen with her mom and Israel, Gracie's boyfriend. They called both of the brothers, the oldest one Nicholas, who was sixteen at the time and the youngest, Andrew, who was fourteen. They both walked in and wondered if they were going to get some good news about their sister. It took Sabrina a while to tell them. But when she did, Nicholas didn't really have anything to tell her. Andrew, the younger brother, hit her. Andrew didn't believe it, and in disbelief ran to his room and started to cry.

This made her really angry. She thought that he would tell her baby that she was a mistake. This got into her mind.

Attending school while pregnant, Sabrina didn't miss a day besides doctor appointments. She stayed in school until the day she went into labor, not like other girls who took a week or two off from school right before their due dates. On the big day, she started getting contractions really early, but waited until Gracie got up to go to work, at around 5 a.m. From there, they headed to the hospital, where Sabrina had her baby girl, Melanie, on January 23, 2009.

Summer Love

ALYSSA MEDINA

Evan Medina, who had dark, wavy hair, 5'9", and 135 pounds, had his first experience with love in the summer of 1985. He acted like a typical seventeen year old. This included hanging out with friends, going to the beach, watching movies, and most of all, listening to his favorite heavy metal bands. Also, he spent time gazing up at the stars and wondering about the meaning of life.

Every other day or so, he went to the local arcade by his house, not only for the games and quality time with his friends, but because it was

Evan Medina

the only place with central air conditioning. They bought snacks and drinks without having to go somewhere else. There, he met Alison, a long, jet black-haired girl. She wore torn jeans with a band shirt and spent all her time going around the arcade playing every game that she hadn't played the day before. When he first laid his eyes on her, he felt a surge of joy, excitement, and nervousness, all at the same time. After a few days of trying to gain the courage to ask her out on a date, he finally did.

He asked her if she would like to go to a beach party with him that Friday. She accepted. On their date, they lay in the sand, talked, ate hot dogs, and swam in the ocean. The more he talked to her, the more he began to realize how much they really had in common. What he loved was not things they had, but all the things they didn't have, in common. They talked for hours.

Alison loved the way Evan's hand fit so perfectly in hers and the way her head rested so beautifully on his shoulder. She liked how he was so polite, respectful, and playful with her, even though they were at his friend's party. She loved how opinionated and passionate he was about almost everything, including politics.

After their date they spent all their time together. They always went to the arcade and played as many games as possible. Sometimes they put a blanket on the grass in his backyard and spent hours gazing up at the stars and talking about aliens and different galaxies. Most of the time, they talked about their lives and childhoods. They did this almost every night until Alison told Evan that she only came to California to visit her relatives. She had to go back home to Arizona at the end of the summer.

Evan, heartbroken that she hadn't told him the truth sooner, didn't know what to do. He felt lost without her now. He knew that he wouldn't be able to hold her soft hand or kiss her beautifully smooth lips anymore. Every day was harder than the day before. He never thought that she would actually leave, especially so soon after she told him. He wanted to make each and every moment he had with her last forever, as did she, but now all they had were the beautiful and romantic memories they made that summer. Alison looked upset and heartbroken every day after she told Evan the truth about the inevitable. She loved Evan and Evan loved her. They wanted to spend the rest of their lives together but they couldn't escape the truth. They were being torn apart.

The day she left, sorrow filled the air and sky. As they said their final goodbyes, tears ran down their faces and their hearts began to separate as though they had been once before.

As he watched her drive away, he began to sob and cry. On his way home all he could think about was her face and the time they spent together. He realized that life without her would be a tragedy and wouldn't be a life worth living. Without her, he would never know what true love or happiness was. He finally understood the saying "it is better to have loved and lost than to have never loved at all".

The Speech Is Toe-Day

MARISSA MEDINA

Leticia Ramirez

In 1972, Leticia Ramirez sat in the kitchen writing a speech for school when her mother asked her to go help her brother carry a Sparklett's glass bottle into the house. As they placed the heavy Sparklett's bottle onto the floor, it slipped out of their hands and fell on her left foot. She yelled out in pain, hopped to the sofa, and pulled off her sock. Her mother screamed in horror because her toe dangled by a piece of skin covered in a huge bubble of blood. Her mother ran to the telephone and called her grandfather. When he got to the house, he gave her a piggy-back ride to his car. Leticia's grandfather sped off to the emergency room. The doctor gave her a shot to numb her foot and sewed her toe back on. She was terrified!

While waiting to be released, she saw a friend from school. Being embarrassed, she felt her face turn bright red. Teary-eyed with a wrapped toe and a splint sticking out from underneath, Leticia hopped out of the doctor's office. When she arrived at her house, she saw her younger brothers and sisters holding little gifts and cards that they hoped would help her feel better and get well soon. She felt so loved by her siblings.

However, she still needed to give her speech the next day. Leticia wore open-toed shoes which made it very hard for her to hide her broken toe from the student body, but she had to try. She thought she would hide her foot behind the podium while she gave her speech. Before she got to the podium, she heard her friend Danny's voice yell out, "Hey, I can see your busted toe!" The audience roared in laughter. Although the podium hid her toe, her peers chuckled and sneered. After the assembly, two friends (one with a broken arm, the other with a broken leg) asked her to eat lunch with them because they were all broken.

Three Days

OSCAR MOJICA

Maria Juarez

Five in the morning. Maria Juarez had to wake up; the time arrived to move to the United States, the land of dreams. She packed two outfits to take on the trip. As she left her childhood memories behind, she heard her mother say, "At God's speed, Maria."

As she arrived at her departure, she noticed the children with their parents. The children, who should have been at home sleeping, had an emotionless expression. Two couples, three families, and five individuals, including her, waited for the pickup van which would take them to the train.

The van arrived. The driver, who had tattoos, cuts, and a bald head, looked like he had been in and out of jail. He commanded, "Get in!"

Everyone got in; my mother entered last. This was the first time she ever left her city, state, and country. She asked, "What's your name?"

"No names!" he shouted. The thirty minute ride through the desert felt like hours, but they finally arrived at the train tracks. The driver said, "The train will be here in a few minutes." My mother heard the train's whistle and looked out into the distance – her future, her dream, and her last hope.

As the train slowed, she and the rest of the group picked up their belongings. They speed-walked to the train. Finally, a man helped the women and children get on the train. It was cold, dark, and empty. They decided to keep the cargo train doors open to have more sunlight. After a couple of hours, the whole group decided to move closer to the cargo doors so they could feel the cold wind. One of the men made a small campfire inside the cargo train to stay warm.

Looking around, a man grabbed a piece of wood; he started to chop it into smaller pieces. Thirty minutes later, they had a fire inside the cargo train. Soon my mom got tired. Even though she was hungry, she decided not to eat the food that she took with her, because she wanted to save it for later. She fell asleep. When she woke up, she saw trees passing like an assembly line. As she sat up, she saw everyone else still sleeping. She decided to go back to sleep to pass time.

BOOM! She woke up to find everyone looking for their belongings and jumping off the train. She was confused. A woman with ghostly eyes looked at her and told her that the police had stopped the train to look for stowaways. Without hesitation, she got her bags and belongings and jumped off the train. She glanced to her right and saw the police. After a long time, she turned left and ran to a new beginning in the United States.

Family Left Behind

LESLY MOLINA

Alma Molina

On 15 November 1983, baby Alma's first cry was beautiful music to Alma Argumedo Molina. She could not believe that she was a mother at 16 years old. But her happiness was short-lived when the doctors soon realized baby Alma had health problems and needed surgery immediately. With an enormous pain in her heart, Alma (mother) signed the papers so her baby could receive the surgery needed. Crying for her baby, she felt like knives were stabbing her in the heart. Nine months had gone by and she was in love with the innocent being inside her womb. Never in a million years would she have thought that only three days after being born baby Alma would pass away due to heart complications. Alma and her boyfriend Elmer Molina were devastated and heartbroken that they had lost their first child and realized they had to plan a funeral.

Years passed. The pain for their lost child became less but it still lingered in their hearts. Soon after, Elmer left Alma to travel up North to find a better job in the United States, to provide a better life for her. Time kept going by and she needed her boyfriend; she became lonely and decided to leave El Salvador to start a life in California. The civil war in El Salvador drove her to move away before the times worsened. Still, she had an emotional attachment to her home country because her baby was buried there. Her family did not want her to leave because they heard much horrible news about emigrating to America and feared that Alma might fall into misfortune. Alma knew she had many things tying her down to her home country, but life in California seemed much better than the life she would offer to her future kids in El Salvador. The picture was painted perfect; her future relied on a land where people, who have never been there, painted it gold. El Norte. She decided to leave. Her journey began on January 7, 1985.

Just like many others, Alma took a bus to Guatemala, where she bought a visa to Mexico. She arrived in El Distrito Federal and spent the night there. Later, the group of people she crossed with caught a train to some other part of Mexico to advance on their journey to "El Norte". Together, Alma and the group kept going. They took a taxi to Tijuana where she waited in hiding to cross the border. When she crossed the border, the coyotes put her and a couple of other people under the seats of a motor-home. After 8½ days of being with people she did not know, Alma reached her destination without any problems. Alma arrived in Los Angeles, California on January 16, 1985. Words cannot express how she felt when she reunited with her soul mate.

Living in Los Angeles, in a room filled with people she had never seen before, scared her, but her mentality was clear. In order to get to the top she had to start at the bottom. She was not privileged enough to get a job and to own a house and a car, like everyone seems to think happens when someone makes it to the United States of America. She did not mind living with other people, but she missed having her own privacy. Alma felt embarrassed to have to ask to borrow the stove and pots to cook a meal. About two years passed, and she became pregnant for the second time, this time with a boy named Elmer Steve Molina, who was born on November 18, 1987.

Years passed, and Alma's father became extremely ill. Living in the U.S., being undocumented, and not being able to sit next to her father during his sickness and agony, killed her emotionally. His body gave out on October 28, 1991. Less than a year later she found out she had the opportunity to become a resident of the United States. She traveled back to El Salvador on January 7, 1992 to complete the process and finalize everything. Ten days later, everything was complete, and she flew back to Los Angeles as a resident.

Innocence Taken Away

BETTY MORALES

Maria De La Cruz Fausto Basulto was born in Guadalajara, Jalisco on March 17, 1967. At the age of fifteen, Maria had the mind of an innocent child. She wasn't allowed to be around boys since her parents were overprotective. If she wanted to get permission to go somewhere, she had to do chores around the house.

At nineteen, she met the love of her life, Oscar Morales, who was also 19. Maria risked getting into trouble with her parents. The risks were worth it because he was able to spend time with her. Maria's mother accepted him, unlike her father, who hated him. He looked at Oscar as a person with no future or potential. Soon, she got tired of her father's constant nagging and negative talk about Oscar. Maria left her house to move in with Oscar. After three years of living together, Oscar cheated on Maria with another woman, Eva, who lived in the neighborhood. After that incident, everything changed. They fought and argued a lot.

After being cheated on, Maria felt devastated. In addition, she did not know that Eva became pregnant. Maria, sad and betrayed, asked her parents if she could move back in with them. They welcomed her back since she was their loving daughter. Two months later, Maria found out she too was pregnant. Oscar had gotten two girls pregnant, but he was unaware of both pregnancies. Once he found out, he decided he wanted to stay with Maria instead of his one night stand, Eva. He was in love with Maria, even though he cheated on her.

Three months later, Maria decided to forgive Oscar and take him back. She knew that raising a baby on her own was going to be difficult, especially with no money or job. Also, the baby needed a father in her life. The main reason she took Oscar back was because she really loved him, and believed that he was her true love. Their lives went back to normal after a while, as if nothing had ever happened. Maria and Oscar moved in together and raised their first child. Finally, after six years, Maria Fausto and Oscar Morales married. They started their new lives when they came to the United States and settled in Boyle Heights, California.

Ten years later, Maria's life changed when she received a phone call. It was a call from a young girl asking for Oscar. Her name was Lupe, and she claimed that Oscar was her father. She wanted to talk to him. Confused at first, Maria became enraged and began yelling on the phone. She demanded to know who it was since she could not believe her story. They argued. Maria told Lupe and Eva not to bother them and to let them live in peace. Eva threatened Maria. She told her that they would never have a happy love life as long as she had anything to do with it.

A Struggle For Change

JESUS OROPEZA

My mother, Silvia Esparza, came to the United States during the 1980s. She emigrated from Zacatecas, Mexico in search of a better lifestyle. Throughout her long journey, my mom witnessed many horrible incidents, which she still carries with her in her darkest memories.

She also learned about different people and their lifestyles while she travelled from Mexico to America. She thought that there were indeed two different worlds. In Mexico, people faced poverty. They were in need of help and change. In the United States, people had more opportunities to succeed.

On her journey, she spent days without food, water, or sleep. She witnessed the deaths of many immigrants like herself, searching for the American Dream. However, she stopped at nothing to make it to her new destination. She believed that whatever did not kill you only made you stronger.

My mother never imagined meeting so many different people on her journey from Zacatecas to the United States. As she learned about other people's backgrounds and struggles, other people had a chance to learn about her's as well. She learned how people left their homelands every day in search of a better life, but she didn't understand why. She also learned how many people died every day, because they get lost in the desert or die of hunger. It was dangerous for women. Many times, they got their belongings and their money stolen or became victims of rape. She felt a connection with these people. They understood each other's rage and pain.

Once in America, she faced the new problem of starting a new life. As an immigrant, my mother wasn't familiar with the city and she didn't speak English. She knew very few people here; my mother was clearly an outsider, but she felt proud of making it to America. Not being able to speak English was a big disadvantage for her. It held her back from several opportunities, mostly jobs, yet she remained strong. She always told herself that life is only as good as you want to make it. She learned and experienced an unforgettable adventure, an adventure that taught her she must lose first before she could win.

Great Expectations

ANGELICA ORTEGA & ELIZABETH FARFAN

She is 36 years old, five feet and two inches tall, with dark black shiny hair that falls down her shoulders like the night sky. Her big green eyes reflect her passion for life, but somewhere in her dark green eyes you can see her sadness. She is thick but her womanly curves symbolize the birth of her two daughters. Her name is Angelica Ramos; she is strong, independent, beautiful, caring, brave, and intelligent.

Angelica lived in Mexico with both of her parents, Jose Luis Ramos Martinez and Maria Del Rosario Hernandez. Her father owned a business where they sold imported American candy like Snickers, Milky Way, and Starburst. Their business became so successful that her dad Jose Luis distributed to smaller businesses and independent companies. They had seven employees. Angelica's dad made approximately five hundred U.S. dollars daily. Angelica was well off; she lived in a big blue house that was separated into three units. At the time she only had one other brother, who was named after her dad, Jose Luis. Later, she had another brother named Juan Diego Ramos.

Angelica, at age eighteen, dropped out of high school because her parents never motivated her to pursue a career or go to college, even though Angelica attended the best private schools in Mexico, including Justo Sierra. Little did she know her life was going to change for the worse.

Being eighteen, she was as happy as she could ever be, vacationing at Mexico's best resorts and dining out in the best restaurants. Angela was spoiled. She couldn't imagine being without her parents, who appeared to be a happily married couple. Her parents married when they were young and restless. Her mom was seventeen years old and her dad was nineteen. Angelica loved her parents and hoped to have a marriage like their's someday.

Although Angelica was still learning and experiencing life, she came to realize that her mother Maria was being unfaithful to her dad Jose Luis.

One warm, sunny Sunday in March, Angelica was at home helping her mother Maria make dinner when the phone rang and startled her. Angelica made her way through the kitchen to the living room where she answered the phone. Her uncle Victor, who was short and weighed about one hundred eighty pounds, with short black hair that was always slicked all the way back, was on the phone.

Uncle Victor asked her, "Mija no sabes donde se fue tu mamá a festejar el 14 de Febrero?"

Angelica replied, "No, tio Victor, no se." Angelica's heart beat faster than usual. She had a gut feeling that things were about to change.

Uncle Victor said, "Tu mamá se fue a festejar con tus primas y llevo a un senor como su acompañante, es su novio se fueron a bailar y a cenar."

Angelica hung up the phone and felt a sudden rush of anger. Angelica thought only of her dad. She marched into the kitchen where her mother was cooking dinner after a long day of work. She was furious and asked her mom to leave.

"Leave," she said.

Screaming at the top of her lungs, Angelica went on, breaking every mirror, lamp, and furniture on her way to her bedroom. Her mother packed her personal belongings from her drawers. Angelica thought back to the nights her mom seemed suspicious, when "going out to a friend's house" was her excuse. Angelica knew then that her mother was cheating on her father.

As her mother left, nervously walking out the door, Angelica grew scared thinking about how her dad would handle the news. Angelica was terrified because she knew her dad owned a handgun and would go after her mom. She cried and cried. She was desperate, lost, confused, and dumbfounded. At long last, Angelica's father arrived home. She spilled her guts and told him everything. She told him about the affair her mother had going on for almost four years, which she had kept a secret, and how she left, replacing her father with some "other guy." Weeks passed by and her father still had the same reaction. He was desperately sad, depressed, frustrated, and full of rage. Angelica's father drank himself to stupidity and gambled his business profit and earnings away. Eventually, he lost every 'peso' he had earned and was hopeless when it came to his long drinking nights at bars. He sold his business, wasting his money on his sleepless nights.

Two weeks later, Angelica's parents decided to give their marriage a second chance. They came to the United States to start a new life, but they failed. Angelica's dad left them in the United States and returned to his home in Mexico City.

Running away from her dark past, Angelica came to the United States from Mexico City when she was twenty-one years old. She was a teenage girl who had big dreams.

The events that occurred in Angelica's life affected her dramatically in the years that followed. To this day, she hasn't been able to let go of the past and seeks to find help someday. Angelica felt the need to have someone by her side to complete her, but failed when she attempted to start a new relationship. In spite of losing her father in a broken marriage, she has her mother Maria with her at times, although she can't help feeling anger toward her mother. She is a tremendously great mother who has raised two wonderful girls on her own, although she misses being in Mexico with her family and friends. She has been successful, with a stable household, and is

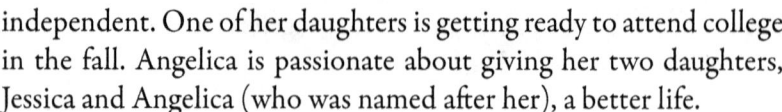

independent. One of her daughters is getting ready to attend college in the fall. Angelica is passionate about giving her two daughters, Jessica and Angelica (who was named after her), a better life.

Summer Days In Boyle Heights

HECTOR ORTEGA

In El Monte, in the summer of the year 1986, Adriana Diaz lived with her mother, father, two sisters, and one brother. It was routine to wake up on a Saturday morning during summer to get ready and visit her family in the Aliso Projects located in Boyle Heights. They visited her Aunt Male's house, where they would meet up with the rest of the family. It was like going to a birthday party every Saturday.

Early in the morning, they woke up, showered and picked their favorite outfit for the day.

Adriana

They got there either by car or bus. If they drove to LA, it took twenty to thirty minutes, but taking the bus was more exciting. They would walk to their starting point, the bus stop at Garvey Blvd. in El Monte, where they would catch the #70 bus. The bus drive was long but nice. It took them about one hour because it went through the streets of El Monte to LA. They saw many different ethnicities as they drove through various cities such as Temple City, Rosemead, Monterey Park and several others. There were many people who would come and go. Adriana and her family were among the few people who stood in the bus for the long ride. The last stop was Cesar Chavez, which was then called Brooklyn Avenue. With much excitement, they walked the four blocks to Mission Road and then to Clarence Street. Finally, they reached their ending point on Via Las Vegas in the Aliso Projects, her aunt's house.

Adriana greeted her aunts, uncles, and cousins. After all the greetings, she went outside with her sister and cousin. They visited their friends and asked if they could walk around the block. They walked around for about two hours before they got hungry and returned to her aunt's house. Once they got back, they saw that more family members had arrived. The female adults and the children walked up the hill to go eat at Jim's Burgers. It was so much fun for her and her cousins to sit alone at a table and pretend to be all grown up. They enjoyed eating and then walking back to the projects. After resting, Adriana went back outside to play. The male adults who stayed behind had started drinking and playing card games. Adriana enjoyed playing cards, too, but became bored after a short while. She often went outside and played kick the can.

Kick the can was Adriana's favorite game, because it was exciting and nerve racking. The game rules were that one person kicked the can and had to get it, while the rest of the players ran to hide. The person with the can had to find the players. The players had to run to the base to be safe. The one who got caught became the next one to kick the can, and so on. Adriana remembers finding the best places to hide and most of the time would be safe. She became sweaty, hot, tired, and filled with relief when she did not get caught. Once the kids got bored of playing kick the can, they played tag. This was Adriana's least favorite game. She hated running. She always got tagged and it was hard for her to tag someone else. Adriana would quit playing that game and shortly after that everyone else also stopped. They then sat on the porch and talked about school, boys, and the funniest part of the day. Since if was still hot in the evening, they needed to freshen up. Adriana and her cousins asked if they could get wet outside. All the parents said yes, and allowed them to play with the water hose. Getting wet on a hot summer night with all her cousins and friends felt great. They were allowed to get wet outside until 9:00 pm and had to dry before re-entering the house. While waiting on the porch, getting dry, Adriana talked with her friends and her cousins. Once dry, she entered her aunt's house to wait for her mother and father to decide to leave. There were times when she spent the night and went home the following day. Most of the time she had to wait until her parents were ready to go. By then she was exhausted and ready for bed. The good thing was that her grandpa was there to drive them home. Sunday morning was another day to visit LA. This is how Adriana spent every summer weekend, full of fun with family and friends.

Success Of A Dream

GEORGINA PORTILLO

Once in the home of Ana, one is delighted by the mouthwatering aroma of a home cooked meal. Ana Centeno lives in Boyle Heights; she is a wife and mother of three daughters. Born in Morelos, Mexico, Ana arrived to the U.S. twenty years ago. She came with nothing and without anyone. Ana was only sixteen at the time, but her age failed to decrease her aspirations for success in the country of possibilities.

When Ana arrived in the U.S., she began working several different jobs. She first began working as a maid for several families in different homes. Then she worked in vegetable packaging, and afterwards as a retailer. Ana struggled through her jobs; none of them paid well or were secure. Ana had a newly formed family to support at that time. At the age of twenty-seven, she switched to working in clothing workshops in downtown, Los Angeles. The pay wasn't any better, but the job was secure. In 2001, Ana decided to start selling gold, in an attempt to make more money and provide for her family, since by then she had birthed her second daughter. She began with small things; she had almost a hundred dollars worth of small rings and earrings. Ana began by selling to her closest friends and apartment neighbors. Those people knew other people who wanted to buy gold, and her clientele grew. Ana began to buy more to expand her stock of jewelry. It highly benefited Ana when people purchased pricier items. She was making a profit and her business was growing successfully.

Ana used the money that she made to rent a house. It was a small home with a single room, and no luxuries. It was still a huge change from the single that her family shared before. Her family was glad to have her and found themselves more comfortable than ever before. After a year of living there, a neighbor, Leticia, came up with an idea for making money. She proposed that Ana could help her sell clothing. Ana suggested that they sell at swap meets as well. Both planned their new business. They began with a few boxes of clothes that they had purchased downtown at wholesale prices. One Saturday, six years ago, Ana and Leticia set a stand at a nearby swap meet. Ana realized that it was a big opportunity to make money and decided it was best to take off on her own. Ana trusted that she could be successful independently.

Ana had her hands full with two businesses. Although she only had an elementary school education, she managed to handle her businesses and make a profit. Ana felt that she was successful and had overcome her limitations. She lived in poverty as a child, had a poor education, and had no family with her when she arrived to the United States. Yet, she managed to do what she herself thought was beyond her capacities. Ana had been successful due to her two small businesses. Every morning, when Ana opened her eyes, she was proud of where she was in life.

As time passed, Ana's profits accumulated in her savings account. Ana began to think of things to treat her family to. Ana felt that it was time to fulfill one of the hopes that she most wanted when she came to the U.S. Ana wished to buy a house for her family. Her biggest reason for deciding this was because of her daughters.

Ana first told her husband that she decided to buy a house. Her husband, Jose, had some trouble with her decision. He felt that buying a home was too much trouble and very expensive. Ana assured him that buying a house was quite easy, plus she had enough for the down payment and all the necessary costs. Jose was still unsure about the plan. Ana told her daughters that she was planning to buy them a house, where they could be comfortable and finally have a yard to play in. All her daughters were overjoyed with her decision. Everyone was excited to find a new home that they would call their own.

Ana began visiting real estate agencies, and signed up with a few. She began to visit homes on sale. Many homes were on sale outside of the city. It took about a year for Ana to find a house that she liked. One day, passing through Boyle Heights, Ana talked about her dream house with her real estate agent. She learned more about prices, units, and space. Ana grew to like the house further once she knew this information.

The real estate agent went with Ana to visit the home on Rivera Street. Ana liked the house and couldn't wait for her daughters to see the house as well. A week afterwards, Ana took her daughters to see the house she had liked, and she eagerly anticipated their opinion. Ana's daughters were fond of the house and felt excited about moving in. That weekend Ana decided to buy the house and called her real estate agent.

Now Ana and her family live contently in their home, which they own. Ana is admired by her daughters, her husband and family. She accomplished so much and began with so little. Ana is most admired and respected by her oldest daughter, Gina, who grew up seeing her parents face life's struggles. After years of hard work, life seems sweet and Ana is happier than ever before. She achieved so much in her few years in the United States.

A Bad Superstition

JULIO PRADO

On a cloudy, cold day, the ground was moist from the previous day's rain. The wind felt like ice cubes touching your skin. Julio Prado had just woken up for work. Waking up on the wrong side of bed made him have a really bad feeling about the day, so he didn't feel like going to work. But, like every other day, his father made him get up and get ready for work. While getting ready in the bathroom, Julio looked at himself in the mirror. He shook his head, because he still had the bad feeling.

Julio was all ready to depart, but before leaving for work, he ate a nice healthy breakfast that his mom had made for him. After leaving the house, Julio rode on the wagon, his favorite way to get to work. Everything looked normal except for that strange feeling. When he got to the road heading to the mango field where he worked, Julio felt even more nervous. The road was slippery. During the ride, Julio forgot about his feeling by singing songs.

When they finally got to the field, he started his normal duties. Everything was going very smoothly until Julio got too close to a bush, and a snake popped out. Julio jumped and his feeling came back. When the snake was about to attack, his father hit the snake with a stick.

Time passed slowly because Julio had that feeling inside him that didn't let him concentrate on his work. After taking a break to relax,

Julio returned to work. He wanted this day to be over as quickly as possible. The good thing was that nothing happened for the rest of the day.

At the end of work, a storm came. Julio jumped on the wagon where the mangos were and left for home. This horrendous day was almost over for Julio. The worst part, though, was about to happen.

The thunder was very loud and the lightning felt really close. The road was very slippery. The thunder grew louder and louder each minute that passed. The horse got scared and started running full speed. It was very hard for Julio's dad to control the beast. A sharp turn was ahead. The horse didn't stop and the wagon flipped, burying Julio under the mangos. Julio father got up really fast looking for his three kids. He found two of his sons. They were okay, but scared. He became anxious because he couldn't find Julio, who was buried under the mangos. Soon Julio's father saw the pile of mangos moving and he started digging. After a few minutes of digging, he finally got to Julio and pulled him out of the pile. He was okay, with just a couple of bruises. Finally, the horse settled down. Julio, his brothers, and his father, who had saved him twice on this day, continued the ride home.

The Path

MARIBEL RAMON

Damia Ramon

In 1984, on a sunny day down in Tepatlaxco Puebla, Mexico, it was just like any ordinary day, where no human being knows what life, or should I say, God, has prepared for her to see. There was a young girl about 3½ feet tall and seven years of age walking barefoot on a road full of dirt, rocks, and broken glass. You can tell that she had walked along the path several times because her body was covered in dust. Her hair was tangled and it had lost its color. Her feet had scars, and right away you could see that her life wasn't a nice road to walk on.

While she was walking, she turned to her right and saw six starving children. They were sitting together waiting for someone, anybody to run up to them and give them food. The girl looked down with a frown and wished she could help, but she couldn't. Then she put her hands over her stomach and grabbed it and noticed that she was starving as well. She continued her walk. Later, the young girl heard a woman yelling; the girl wondered and turned to her left and witnessed a couple fighting and saying unnecessary comments about each other. The girl saw the couple's children's eyes full of tears, fearing that maybe something worse could happen between them. She knew the man would soon leave and the children would turn sad because the father was never coming back. She didn't know why but she felt overcome with sadness as she knew that the man would probably be happy with some other woman, while the family was left behind, destroyed and depressed.

The girl started to walk with her shoulders forward. Her back curved almost like a humpback, and her knees were bending down as if they were giving up on her. She was tired, tired of walking or tired of her life going to the same path.

The hot sun burnt her smooth, honey color tone, leaving her looking like bacon. She decided to rest under the shadow of a tree. Massaging her feet, she noticed that she was bleeding. How could she not notice? Was she ignoring it? Ignoring the pain of her feet? Or the pain within her heart because she felt alone on this difficult path.

After cleaning the blood off her feet, she had two cuts from the broken glass. Would she be scarred? Maybe. Scarred in her soul? Probably. She ripped half of her shirt and wrapped it around her feet. After caring for her injury and resting for a while, she stood up and started to walk again as if nothing happened.

Leaving footprints along the path, she kept walking forward. There was neither turning back nor a hesitating move. She wondered who was guiding her on this path of memorable moments and life experiences. Was it God, destiny, or herself? It's just the cycle of life, she said.

Once she made a right turn, she saw a hardworking woman working in the fields under the hot sun. The woman looked tired and struggled to stand up after being on her knees for hours. However, from miles away she noticed sparkles in the woman's eyes -- the sparkle of hope. She saw a girl about the same age as herself standing in front of the woman and at that particular moment, the world stopped for a second, and she realized that the woman's hope was her one and only daughter. Just by being a witness to that incredible moment, she had received the juice of happiness and joy that filled her heart. She felt the mother's love hugging her, too. This was something she had been waiting for, walking through this ugly path that's called life. With a beautiful smile on her face, she gladly kept on walking, knowing that there was someone out there looking after her. She was safe.

The Lack Of
A Better Future

ANTHONY ROMO

Like many women, my mother had to work extremely hard to raise five children. Elva Peña, a woman of about 5'8", worked as a "costurera" (seamstress), and made sports clothes. At the start of 2007, business started to decline so she started to worry about her children. In her mind, she wanted to go to the United States to have a better future and life by securing a better education for her children. She tried to obtain a visa, but the U.S. Consulate denied her. Still, she decided not to give up and stuck with her decision.

In June of 2007, my mother found another way to cross the border, even though this was not the ideal one. She decided to pay a "coyote" to help her. Days later, on a sunny Sunday afternoon at about 4:00 p.m., my mother took an airplane from Mexico City to Tijuana to begin her journey. She took her two younger children, including a daughter, leaving behind two other sons. Her daughter, Ivonne, was wearing blue jeans and a black shirt with a white skull on it. Once they got to Tijuana, "La Guera", a friend of my grandmother, gave them shelter for three days. After that, Elva and her children were going to try to cross the border.

My uncle Carlos had recommended a "coyote" to my mother. He said that in the years that this coyote had been crossing people over to the U.S., he had never been caught. So my mother trusted him and followed his advice. As soon as she stepped out of La Guera's house,

Elva had a feeling of insecurity. She and her children had to walk about twenty minutes to meet with the "coyote." On her way, she saw numerous poor, dirty people and houses that did not even look like houses. They looked like they were made of cardboard and sticks, as if someone would just be there for one night. There was also an odor of trash with human waste all over Tijuana. She thought about all this, and she didn't want her children to end up like the inhabitants of those "houses." The sight made her more determined to cross the border, but at the same time she wondered what her little kids were feeling. Their faces had expressions of sadness, anger, happiness, and frustration, all at the same time. Elva also wondered what her life would be like in the U.S. Would it be better than in Mexico? Would she be happy in her new home? Many questions like these popped up in her head, but for now none of them had an answer. She and her children kept walking down the street and Elva had the feeling that everyone had their attention on them, as if the people from Tijuana knew what they were going to do, as if they had done something really horrible.

Once Elva met with the "coyote", they started talking about the price for crossing the border, how they were going to cross and how secure it would be, the probabilities of being caught, and what would happen if they got caught. My mother asked the "coyote" all kinds of questions to make sure her children would be fine through that process. After two hours or so, they came to an agreement. My mother, who is a very smart business woman, made a good deal. She ended up paying one thousand- five hundred dollars per person, which meant six thousand dollars for the four of them. The "coyote" originally said that they had to cross one by one, but my mother disagreed with that because she had heard many stories of kids being kidnapped while crossing the border. The "coyote" gave my mother another option to cross two by two, one little kid and one adult. Elva accepted this option because she felt more secure about it. The "coyote" also said that the crossing would be really secure. Elva said, "Okay, I will pay you once you have gotten us over, but if you don't, forget about your money." He agreed and they shook hands.

On the U.S. side of the border, my uncle Joaquin had to wait for news about my mother and the decision she had made. He had the money to pay the "coyote".

That night, at about 11:00 p.m., my mother and my siblings prepared to cross. My mother saw her children shiver as the wind touched their delicate skin. Elva told them to wear something warm because the night was going to be very long.

Once with the "coyote," they had to follow his instructions. He told Elva to go in the trunk of the black car in the garage with one of the children. Then he told the same thing to her daughter Ivonne. After that, he covered them with a white blanket.

They were approaching the border quite fast. Everything seemed to be okay, until they were stopped by the border patrol. The customs officer asked the "coyote" to open the trunk. So he did it.

They captured my mother and her child, but the "coyote" escaped. After some hours, the border patrol released them in Tijuana. My mother, with determination on her face, decided not to give up, so she tried it again the next night. They went through the same process from beginning to end. But this time Elva felt they would be successful. Once in the trunk, a drop of water rolled down the side of Elvas's right cheek and ended up on the forehead of her child. He turned to her and saw her tearing up. Elva hugged her son, Emiliano, as if this would be the last time they would see each other. She was also praying in a low whisper. Emiliano felt nervous. Emiliano did not understand what was happening. He put his arms over his head trying to hide from the border patrol. He asked Elva what was happening, why she was shaking so hard, and why she was so pale. Elva just kept hugging her son and told him, "No te preocupes mijo; todo va a estar bien" ("Don't worry, everything will be fine"). They were once again in line to cross, but this time she had more luck and they passed without incident. No check point. No stop. No border patrol. Not anything.

My mother felt an internal peace and satisfaction. Once on the other side, the "coyote" brought my mother and her three children to my Aunt Patty's house in Los Angeles. Aunt Patty is my mother's sister. They arrived in L.A. at about 10:00 p.m. My uncle Joaquin paid the "coyote" the six thousand dollars and the "coyote" left. The next morning, my mother was surprised because she discovered that Los Angeles, California, looked just like her home town, with old houses, trash on the streets, and stores like in Mexico. Even some of the streets looked like the ones in Mexico. She said, "If you go to downtown LA, you might feel like you're in Mexico because of the way the streets look, with all those 'puestos.'"

She started to look for a job right away to bring her two other sons to join her. After six months she made that happen. This decision was important for her and her children because here her children have more opportunities for everything, and can also be bilingual.

An Immigrant's Dream

ADRIANA SALAS

Jose Salas

Jose Salas, my dad, was born near the sierra at Durango, Durango, Mexico where four brothers and a sister joined him on his everyday journey. My dad is the second to last son. As a child, he had a rough life. His dad wasn't the greatest dad a child could have. But even though my dad's life was not the greatest, he became a great dad. My dad is an extremely unique person in the way that he gives us advice.

On November 29, 1985, a regular autumn day, my dad crossed the border to choose a better life for his family and for his future family. Being new to a country was the scariest feeling in the world. My dad never knew what he might encounter. My dad remembers seeing enormous buildings that illuminated the night sky, and people walking up and down the perfectly shaped streets. Mesmerized by so many things, my dad also remembers that on the day he got to the United States people were celebrating an American holiday known as Thanksgiving. My dad traveled with a friend of his who got them a place with his aunt, who lived in Los Angeles, California. The location of the house was in East Los Angeles, on the famous Whittier Blvd. The aunt of my dad's friend lived in a small house with one bedroom, a bathroom, a kitchen, and a small living room. Getting to the house became the easiest part; getting a room to sleep in was a problem. There were about twenty-seven people, including the landowner herself, living there. The garage was also used as a residence. The first night was almost impossible to rest, far away from his home. My dad missed his family and for the first time his life became weird and scary. Going back was not an option. Staying and continuing to move forward was the only choice my dad had at the moment.

The next morning my dad woke up hearing noises. The other people living in the house were getting up as their everyday routine. At first my dad got confused, for he didn't recognize where he was, but the most confusing part was that he didn't get why these people were getting up as early as two in the morning. Little did my dad know that the same fate would be in store for him. After the group of people left, my dad went back to sleep. He didn't see the purpose in staying awake. By late morning, a friend's friend gave them directions to a restaurant that needed employees. My dad's first job was at a burger place. There he learned how to cook burgers and burritos, but the restaurant was a fast paced workplace that my dad couldn't keep up with. Cooking food was not a man's job, according to my dad. This job only lasted about a week. After that he went from one job to another. My dad also worked on the streets, selling corn, fruits, vegetables, and tamales. He worked for a whole year, day and night. During this year, it became more and more difficult to get money. Standing in the cold, rainy weather and then on hot sunny days was something my dad hated, but he didn't have a choice. Then, in 1986, a friend of my dad got him a job at a meat packing house where the owner of the company liked his efficiency and work and told him that the job was all his. In 1987, the same company promoted him to become a truck driver. As the years went by, his skills as a truck driver became stronger. My dad was able to get his citizenship and was also able to gain a Class T driver's license to drive commercial and private trucks. Now my dad works for Athens Industries, where the pay is good enough so we can get by as a family. Also, he is able to support his family in México. His first marriage was the result of getting his citizenship. My dad says, "If I had the power to go back in time and do the process once again, I would do it."

As the years passed by, my dad never stopped believing in himself, and I admire him for that.

"Coming to the United States was a life changing experience. You never know what to expect. Yes, I was scared, but I was willing to sacrifice for the ability to stay in America," says my dad.

This Story Is Dedicated To Both My Parents
& In Loving Memory of Jesus Felix

A Ticket To America

MICHELLE SALINAS

While watching Mickey Mouse cartoons, young Maria Elena fantasized about meeting Mickey Mouse one day. She constantly created images in her head of strolling around the Walt Disney theme park, of waving hello to the princesses, and of blowing kisses to the handsome princes. On the other hand, by age eight, she only saw Disneyland as a far, far away dream. Thus, Maria Elena gave up on this fantasy, not knowing that it would reappear twelve years later, once she married Jose. This fantasy would later symbolize more than just a trip to the "happiest place on Earth."

Maria Elena

Since Jose already lived in the United States, Nena (as everyone called her) decided to join him. Three months after their wedding, the couple left Mexico for the United States, where Jose already had a job waiting for him. While riding the train, they passed through rich green vegetation and mesmerizing fields: the great outdoors. While Jose napped, Nena stepped outside onto the train's balcony. The fresh breeze caressed her face and whispered into her long, wavy, blonde hair. As the train raced through the fields, loose soil flew towards Nena's face, causing her to sneeze a few times. Soon, she realized that she had never inhaled such fresh air before, as she had lived in the city her entire life. Suddenly, she thought about how far from home the train had already traveled, and a sense of freedom ran through her.

The train raced through the country all the way to Tijuana, border town between Mexico and the United States. As Nena stepped off of the train and onto the Mexican soil, she realized that she would soon step into a foreign land. The moment finally arrived; the newlyweds entered the United States of America.

Weeks passed, Jose continued to work as he had done all his life, but Nena became nostalgic for her home, her family, her job, and her friends. She missed the citric smell of her father's homemade orange juice as it lingered in her nose and memory, the sweet strawberry flavor of her sister's homemade milkshakes, and the loud and goofy laughter of her friends while they waited for her to get off work. Nena longed for the people and places of Mexico and the soothing sounds of Spanish as it floated through the air. Most importantly, Nena wanted to simply hug her father Papa Pancho, mother, and siblings. She confessed her nostalgic feelings to Jose, but he struggled to understand her because she had been very excited when they had left Mexico. After much persuading and pleading, he finally decided to pay for Nena's train back home.

Back home, her family jumped with joy over her unexpected and quick return. Tears of joy rolled down her cheeks as she hugged her daddy once again, her sisters and brothers, and, of course, her mother. Once again she heard Spanish words echo through the living room as her family conversed with excitement. She smelled her father's orange juice being prepared in the kitchen, and savored the unmistakable taste of her sister Chela's strawberry milkshake when she took a sip. She began to question whether she had the courage to again leave everything that she had known.

Exhausted by the trip, Nena escaped the noise by wandering back into her room. There, she found one of her younger cousins watching a Mickey Mouse cartoon. Suddenly, memories flooded back into Nena's mind. Sitting next to her cousin Lolita, Nena stared at the little black and white mouse that had been so present during her childhood dreams. She recalled how desperately she wanted to one day visit that little mouse's home, that home called Disneyland. Then Nena remembered that she had given up on that fantasy because she never thought she would ever be able to travel to Disneyland. Different thoughts entered her head; connections were made. Nena thought and thought. Finally, she came to a conclusion.

A month later, Maria Elena departed from her homeland once again, but this time sure of her decision. Jose received her with a huge hug and kiss and a great surprise. He handed Nena two tickets, tickets that read "Disneyland Theme Park." She screamed while tears ran down her cheeks.

At that moment, Nena travelled back in time to her childhood. At Disneyland, she ran around taking photos with every Disney character. Nena dragged Jose around the theme park a million times. They watched all the parades on "Main Street" and listened to the magical music of the passing carriages. She especially loved the attraction of "It's a Small World" because the mechanical dolls greeted her in Spanish. Finally, her lunch consisted of a typical American burger, fries, and soda.

That is when all became clear for Maria Elena. This great sacrifice paid off. Her childhood dream of meeting Mickey Mouse in person came true and she thought about her future children. Maria Elena now dreamed of having children and she knew that her kids' dreams would be immense. All their dreams would come true if she stayed in the "land of opportunities."

My Dad's Dream

ABRAHAM SANABRIA

It was a hot, clammy, and tiring Monday in September. It started out like every other Monday. My dad Gonzalo, who was about fifteen years old, woke up at 5:30 a.m. to leave the little house he lived in and met with his friend at the panaderia by his block. After meeting, they started their long road that they always took to get to the field where they had been working for a little over a year now. On their walk, they passed through the city they lived in, then through other farms and fields. Every Monday they left, and they came back on Thursday. The owner of the field, who also happened to be their boss, allowed them to sleep in the little, worn out barn he had so that they could wake up and get to work sooner. On their journey to the field, they always came across this old, worn out field that looked as if nobody owned it and there were always these crows that would hang out in the shade. When they approached the crows they always flew away, so nothing ever caught their attention. But this day something they didn't expect happened.

That day, one of the crows walked up to them as they were walking. It was a big crow with a gray spot by its left eye. Its wings looked old. It also seemed bigger than the others, but that might have been because it was closer than the rest. As my dad looked closer, he noticed something about the crow. Its eyes reminded him of something or someone. As my dad and his friend saw how it walked up to them without hesitation, they thought it was hungry and wanted some bread, so my dad threw a piece at the crow. It didn't even look at the bread as it hit the ground a few inches away. They didn't notice anything strange, so they continued on their way towards the crow, but as they got closer they saw that it wouldn't move. The crow was holding its ground. When they were about a foot away the crow let out a thunderous caw. It was not a scornful caw. It was more like a consoling caw that sounded as if it was trying to speak. They had never heard a sound like that come out of a bird, but they just carried on. They had to get to work.

As soon as they got there they quickly noticed that their boss was cheerful. He was never cheerful. He was always walking around with a bitter look on his face, as if every step he took was extremely aggravating. There was never a day when he wasn't harsh to one of his workers, but something about this day was different. That whole day felt as if it flew by, and not in a tiring way, but as a good day. As my dad headed to the barn for sleep he was already starting to notice all the strange things happening around him. Even as a teenager, my dad has always thought the same way. He felt that if things were going well it was just a sign that something bad was headed his way. It went on the same for the next day; his boss was in a good mood. After he was done he went to the barn to relax for a little. That night, he had a dream:

As a ten year old, he was playing outside in front of the house when he noticed one of those green taxis right in front of his home, waiting. He heard footsteps and quickly saw his dad walking towards the cab. He called his dad but his dad didn't hear him, so he ran after him. As he got to the cab, his dad was already closing the back door. He shouted at his dad.

Finally, his dad turned and Gonzalo asked him, "¿A donde vas?"

His dad answered, "Ya me tengo que ir. Te amo."

In his dream my dad was scared. He remembers feeling as if he was awake.

As my grandfather told him, "I love you," my dad quickly

responded, "¿Puedo ir contigo?", which means, "Can I go with you?" At this point his dad said, "A donde voy no puedes venir, quida a tu madre." He told his son that where he is going, the son cannot go and that he must take care of his mother.

At that moment my dad told me that the taxi started moving slowly and that he was holding on to the window where his dad was. Soon the car started going a little faster and my dad was running beside the cab calling his father as loud as he could until he couldn't keep up. When he woke up he remembered having tears rolling down his cheeks.

He didn't pay attention to his dream. He just took it as a nightmare and went back to sleep. Those next four days kept being better than the last. He ended up getting to count the baskets instead of picking the fruit, which was like a raise. When he came home on Friday, he wished he had stayed at work. As soon as he got home his mother was waiting for him outside. She ran to him and had to tell him what he already felt in the back of his mind, even though he had refused to pay attention to it. She told him that his father had gotten really sick on Monday and that he passed away on Wednesday morning. They both were crying as she said those words. He never told any of his family about his dream. He had kept it secret for all these years.

David's Memories

DAVID SANCHEZ

As David got ready to go to his friend's house he wouldn't have guessed that he would find the woman that he would one day marry, Martha. These two people came from the same place. Both were born in Puebla, Mexico and lived close to each other. Still, as children they had not paid any attention to each other. They had gone to the same school and had seen each other at times. Three years later, when both were in California, on a day when David went to his friend's house, he began to pay attention to her.

David and Martha Sanchez

David spoke to Martha through phone calls. He knew she was home because of her brother. When David first came to California, he and Martha's brother talked. One day he told David that Martha came to California, so David asked for their home number.

They talked to each other by the phone and he said, "I'll be going to visit you at your home," and she said, "Okay."

As he went to her house they started talking. He asked, "When did you come here to California?"

"It's been a month since I arrived."

He then asked, "Where are you working?"

She said, "I work at sewing."

They started liking each other so they continued talking. Every day they spoke to each other. Later, they would go together and take a walk at the park, sometimes even catch a movie. Before all that, when David again saw Martha in California, he was too shy to talk to her and felt nervous, yet he wanted to talk to her. He wanted to try to get to know her. They were together for eighteen months and at the end of that time they decided to get married.

He was only twenty-two years old. The wedding was small and only had a few guests. David and Martha lived a simple life with some problems along the way. They had their share of hardships but many good times.

Martha became sick with cancer in February of 2000, and one day Martha had to go to the hospital. That day, when she went to the hospital, David took his son to go see his mother. Later on, he also took his daughter. It was painful for him and for the rest of his family, but he tried to be strong for them. David was able to stay there longer than his children. The next day his wife passed away.

When he was young, David never saw himself taking care of two children alone and being a widower in his early life. He saw himself taking care of his children with a wife and growing old with a wife. So many things have happened in David's life, both excellent and unfair. He met Martha and got married to her. They had two children. They spent so much time with each other, first as friends, then as a couple, and finally as a married couple. The bad thing is that they had fights with each other, and that they had financial problems. But they continued on with each other and with their children.

A Physical And Emotional Struggle

JUAN SIBRIAN

In the early 1960's, in the month of October, Domitila was born. Domitila's family was so poor that there were days they'd only eat tortillas. Domitila and her older brother, Felipe, would go to work in the farm fields and pick corn, carrots, and other crops.

They often worked for little money. As they grew up they couldn't afford to go to school, so they dropped out at a young age. Domitila had to find a new job to support her family. As Domitila grew up, she worked as a housekeeper. She started working with "Gringos" at a young age, and did stuff that needed to get done around the rich people's houses. For years she did that, making enough to support her brothers and sisters. As her siblings grew up, they all found jobs to help support each other. By the age of eighteen she had saved enough money to migrate to the United States. Luckily, she had family she could live with in the United States.

In the meantime, Domitila was exploring this new world. In Los Angeles, California, housekeeping was the thing she knew best. As the years passed, she met friends and started to go out and have fun. During those years she didn't date anyone until the age of twenty-eight when she met this handsome man who, with just the look of his eyes, made her fall in love.

Domitila and Juan went out for a couple of years. They didn't want to get married until they had kids. After three years together,

Domitila became pregnant. Luckily, Juan was a truck driver who made enough money to support the family. As the years passed by, they had two more kids, Oscar and Rocio, who followed the eldest, Juan Jr.

Domitila started noticing that Juan's attitude changed. He wouldn't come home some nights. So Domitila did a little investigating of her own and found out that Juan had other kids with another woman.

Domitila became a mother and father for her three children. She worked late at night during the weekends as a waitress to put food on the table. For the following years, Domitila struggled at being a single mom, so she went to the welfare office to ask for help. As the kids grew up, they got summer jobs while going to school. They made enough money to buy their own stuff so Domitila wouldn't have to spend money on them. Also, her kids gave her money to help buy stuff that was needed around the house. As they grew up, Domitila stayed home alone while the kids went to school.

Domitila had great kids who weren't into negative activities. The second youngest son played football at Roosevelt High School. Her youngest daughter was in her first year in high school. As time went by, Juan, her oldest son, noticed that his mom needed a partner, someone who could make her happy, make her laugh, and take her out to places. She met someone at her workplace. Little by little, Domitila started going out with a wonderful guy name Jose Luis. In time, Domitila introduced Jose Luis to her kids, and they all started going out as a family to the movies and other places. Domitila noticed that her children got along pretty well with her new boyfriend. She also noticed that he was good with kids. As time passed, Domitila's oldest son Juan noticed a change in his mother: that she was happy, and had nothing to worry about with Jose Luis on her side. After dating Jose Luis for four years, Domitila was shocked when Jose Luis proposed to her. These were the best three minutes of her life, Domitila later told her kids.

A Mother's Struggle

EDUARDO SIMENTAL

Back in 1993, Yolanda Simental relaxed in her bed, watching television and rocking her second born child side to side. The entire room was overwhelmed with warmth from the love Yolanda gave to her baby. Yolanda lay in her bed, tired but with enough energy to wiggle Eduardo's tiny hand and tickle his enchanting stomach.

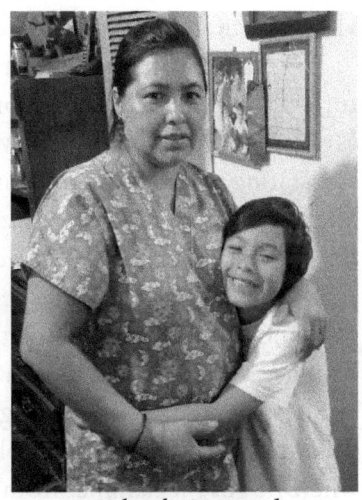

Yolanda Simental

The first born child, Jose Simental, watched television along with Yolanda, but quietly slipped out of the bed and opened the door to explore the living room. Curious, little Jose grabbed picture frames and sticks that lay on the ground. Jose went under the table, passing from chair to chair looking for any interesting object. From one of the chairs, Jose found a hammer lying next to the wall behind the chair. He attempted to pick up the hammer, but clearly found out that the hammer weighed more than what a one year old could handle. Not able to think about the consequences, Jose picked up the heavy tool and started wobbling towards the kitchen door. Then, he walked through the kitchen, passing the refrigerator and oven. He reached the end of the kitchen, getting a hold of the doorknob and twisting. Jose moved his miniature legs past Apartment 3, then Apartment 1. He finally completed a left turn to Apartment 2.

Jose knocked on the door softly, but nobody seemed to open. Suddenly, he banged on the entrance until a drunken man opened the door. At first, he grinned at Jose, then, laughing at Ramon Simental who was with him, he told him that his son had arrived, while he took a drink of his beer. Ramon seemed surprised to see Jose until he saw the hammer clutched in his hand. He instantly became engulfed with anger and stormed out of the apartment, passing Rooms 1 and 3 with his beer still in his hands. Ramon reached Apartment 4 and violently entered.

Yolanda remained cozy, with Eduardo sleeping by her side. She turned to see the bedroom door slam open with the drunken Ramon furiously standing in the doorway. Yolanda, dumbfounded, lay in bed just staring at him, watching him prepare his arm to launch the beer. She moved to the side to protect her baby. The beer can barely missed her and Yolanda quickly jumped out of bed and yelled, "Why did you throw that at me? You could've hit my baby!"

Ramon yelled back, "Why the hell did you let Jose out with the hammer, are you stupid or what?"

She responded, "I'm nursing Eduardo and the last time I saw Jose was when he walked out to play in the living room. I don't know where he got the hammer from or how he got to you!"

Ramon mumbled, "You're just irresponsible," but was quickly interrupted by Yolanda

"How can I be irresponsible when I am being a mother? You are the idiot; you're out partying and getting drunk with your friends. You aren't fit to be a parent!"

He charged towards her, ready to strike her. Full of courage, Yolanda started punching and kicking him, preventing him from getting any closer to Eduardo. He then overpowered her and dropped her on the bed. Yolanda moved her hand around the bed and found the beer can.

She clutched the can in her hand and smashed the container against his head. Ramon fell to the ground, dazed with blood pouring out of a gash above his eye.

Yolanda glanced at Eduardo and told Ramon, "Don't you ever harm me and don't ever hurt my children. I swear I will use every bit of my strength to protect my babies and myself." Yolanda watched Ramon slowly stand on his feet and walk out of her sight. She walked to the kitchen and found Jose walking in from the outside. Yolanda picked him up and carried him to the bedroom. Yolanda held Jose and Eduardo while replaying the fight in her thoughts. She would do anything to keep her children safe, even if it meant facing the people she loved.

The Surprises Of Life

ESTHEFANIE SOLANO

Gabriel

As he walked alone through the scorching hot desert, Gabriel couldn't help but replay in his mind the dreadful series of events that led him towards his decision to finally cross the border.

Everything started in the hot summer of 1991. Gabriel and his family lived in a two-story house about a block away from the apartments and retail stores his father had given him the day of his wedding. He rented the locations out to several different families but had been thinking of moving from Colima to Guadalajara to be closer to his daughter who had moved there after getting married. Of course, all of this was still merely an idea.

Near the end of the month, just like every other time, he asked his daughters to go out and collect the monthly rents from the apartment and store tenants. However, when his daughters arrived at each location, many of the tenants refused to pay the rent that was owed for the month. They wouldn't say why, just that they needed to speak with Gabriel before giving them any more of their money.

~

When his daughter Ana arrived at a family friend's house, she told Ana that she heard the neighbors talk about getting together against their family because someone had told them Gabriel was putting the locations up for sale and kicking them out without notice. They claimed that if Gabriel was going to sell the properties, they should have been the first to be notified in order to have time to look for a new place to live or try to gather enough money to buy the property.

Ana was shocked at hearing the news. As far as she knew, her dad had never thought about selling the locations. Gabriel had always been kind to the residents of his apartments, giving them fair rental rates and repairing any problems that occurred. She confronted her dad and told him about the events that had transpired. He could not believe the tenants were aware of this! He had only mentioned it to a few of his personal friends. The very next day, Gabriel decided to move forward and start the sale of the property. He wasn't wasting any time. As soon as the sun rose he was out of the house and off to look for a realtor. He came across a small office not ten minutes away from where he lived. He walked in and was quickly greeted by a young gentleman. Gabriel wanted to make this sale as soon as possible. He could not wait to get out of Colima. Before he left, they set up an appointment to go look at the location the following day.

Arriving at the location the following day, the realtor began to take pictures of the apartments and stores and their surroundings. He was definitely pleased to see it was all in very good condition. He assured Gabriel that selling it would take no time. However, if he wanted the sale to be as quick as possible, Gabriel needed to go to his office where he had the paperwork finished and sign it so it was on file and ready for when someone made an offer for the properties.

The following week, Gabriel was called in to sign all the paperwork he had been told about. Unfortunately, Gabriel was a very trusting man and signed all the paperwork without bothering to read it -- something he would soon regret. After signing, the realtor said he would notify him as soon as an offer was made.

About a month passed and he still hadn't heard back from the realtor. Gabriel decided to look for him to get a report of how the process was going, but before he could leave, one of his daughters came into the house running and screaming. They no longer had anything! When Gabriel finally got her to calm down, she said that when she went to try to collect the rent for the month from the few people who still willingly paid it, the tenants told her that a young man had been coming around during the past weeks and had sold the houses and stores to individual renters for a very low amount of money. At that moment, Gabriel didn't know what to believe. But for a moment he felt relieved. The realtor didn't have the authority to sell anything! He wasn't the owner! However, the image of him signing "Gabriel Soltero Velazquez" without a second thought came into his head and hit him like ice cold water. He felt he had let everyone down. How could he have signed something without thinking?

After the incident, all he thought about doing was running to the "realtor's" office and strangling him for being a slimy snake. Everything he felt was portrayed in his face so no one allowed him to leave the house. The following day, two of his daughters went with him to the police station to try and see what they could do about all of this mess. They told him that if he had signed a deed over to the "realtor," they would have to settle the situation in court and it would be Gabriel's word against the realtor's.

When the police went looking for the realtor, it was too late. He had left Colima and no one seemed to know his whereabouts. Without the realtor, Gabriel was unable to regain the ownership of the properties and the sale of the houses went on without him being able do anything about it

Months after losing the properties, paying the bills became harder and harder, and cutting back the expenses was becoming too much. Without the extra money that used to come from the houses, Gabriel and his family were barely making ends meet. It pained him to see how drastically his family's lives had changed, and he was ashamed of not properly providing for his family. He believed the only way to make life easier was to emigrate to the United States to get a better

~

job. He jumped at the first opportunity that came his way.

Now Gabriel found himself in the middle of a hellish desert so far away from home and so far away from his destination, unsure if this was the right decision or not. Something up ahead caught his attention. The sand made everything blurry and hard to define but he had to make out that sight no matter what. Just a few feet away stood the fence that divided him and his family's future.

Always Remember

JOSEPH TORRES

My mom's name is Ana Torres. She always dreamed of coming to the United States, and at the age of seventeen, she decided she wanted to come. She heard that there were better opportunities here, and one could live a better life.

My mom never imagined herself coming to the United Sates. She never had a plan to come. She lived in D.F. Mexico with her grandmother. She never met her mom. She talked to my aunt in the United States, who would tell my mom to come over. That's when my mom started making plans.

She was pregnant at that time with my older sister. She debated with herself whether to go or not. She really didn't want to leave, but something went through her mind that told her she should go. So she told my dad that she wanted to come to the U.S. because she wanted to study. She always desired to go to school. She started making plans with my aunt to go to the U.S. and finally both my parents and my aunt settled on the day. My mom found a person that would help them pass the border.

One of my mom's friends told her that she knew of a group of people who were going to jump the border, and that there was going to be a guy on the other side with a car to drop them off in Los Angeles. My aunt said that once they reached Los Angeles to give her a call and she would pick them up and give them a ride to her house. My mom was living at her grandmother's house at the time. She didn't want to tell her grandmother that she was coming to the U.S. because she was scared that her grandmother would hit her or do something so she wouldn't be able to come. My mom didn't take any chances. She packed her stuff as fast as she could and took off to my dad's house.

The group was going to depart the next night. The following day marked a big step for my mom. She was really scared because she didn't know what it was going to be like. She also worried because she was pregnant and didn't want anything to happen to the baby. My mom was really nervous. She and my dad went where the group was going to gather. The leader was already there as were a few other people. The group started moving. She tried to stay positive and just think about the benefits.

The group started heading to the desert. When they got to the desert, she was told to be quick. They were running as fast as they could, but my mom couldn't really run because she was pregnant. It was really hard going through the desert because there were holes in the ground and her feet got stuck in some. Fortunately, my dad helped her get unstuck. My mom felt really tired after walking for miles. She had rocks inside her shoes and they were hurting her.

When the guy leading the way said they were almost there, my mom got scared that she might have to jump something. The guy leading the way said that they would help her get over the border. My mom was cautious about it, but she was willing as long as they helped her. They kept running, until they saw the border. My mom looked back and something went through her mind. If she went to the United States, she and her baby would have a better life. They got to the border, and everybody tried helping her jump it. They still had to walk for a while until they reached the van taking them to safety.

They saw the driver waiting for them and they all ran to the van. My mom entered the van first and then everybody followed. They headed to Los Angeles, and my mom asked the driver if he had a phone. He did, so my mom called my aunt, informing her that they were out of Mexico. My aunt was really happy that everything went well. My aunt told my mom to go to Spring Street and 6th when they got to LA. The van was full of cheers. Everyone was happy they were going to see their families. Both of my parents were happy. Everything looked different to my mom. For her it was something beautiful, a place where she would have better opportunities, but she was really tired, so she decided to take a nap.

My dad woke her up when the driver said they were almost there. She woke up to the bright lights of downtown Los Angeles. It was a beautiful place and she quickly fell in love with Los Angeles. The driver dropped off the people and everyone came out of the van and said farewell. My mom asked the driver if he knew where Spring Street and 6th was. He told her it was only two blocks away. Once again, using the driver's phone, my mom called my aunt, telling her they were now in Los Angeles. My aunt told my mom that she was already there waiting for them. My aunt and my mom were happy because they were finally going to see each other. My mom and dad went running to Spring and 6th streets. When my mom saw my aunt, she started crying because she never imagined this moment happening. My aunt and my mom discussed how everything went. As they were leaving for my aunt's house, my mom looked up at the sky and said, "Thank you, Jesus, for bringing us safely and giving us a chance to do something for our lives and the life of my baby."

A Road Of Sadness

CRISTIAN UMANZOR

In mid-April of 1986, Gladys Umanzor, a short, skinny, light-skinned woman, packed a couple of small bags. She packed clothes, water, and memories from her days of infancy. She prepared herself for a journey she would never forget, from El Salvador to the United States.

The day her journey began, she gathered and united with nine other Salvadorians from La Union, her hometown.

Gladys and company crossed to their first destination, Guatemala. Guatemala borders El Salvador, so crossing wasn't very difficult. The group spent three long days in a house where they just ate, bathed, and slept. At night, Gladys kept thinking about her struggles growing up, especially one in particular, the Salvadorian Civil War. All the terrifying, bloody images she witnessed tormented her, but they also motivated her to continue her pursuit for exile away from the destruction.

The three days passed quickly. Gladys and the rest of the group continued their journey. Before they knew it, they had crossed all of Guatemala and found themselves with a bigger challenge. Gladys had to cross the river dividing Mexico and Guatemala. As she crossed, the river's cold water crept up her legs and the images from the war suddenly haunted her once again. Her motivation level increased drastically and she whispered to herself, "I'm one step closer." Tired and breathless, Gladys and the rest finished crossing the river and entered Mexican territory.

A truck waited for them minutes away from where they finished crossing the river. Very uncomfortable and anxious to get out of the car, they were transported to Hermosillo, where they spent a night at their guide's friend's house. The night went by and morning arrived. It was time to keep moving.

Crossing Mexico took two weeks and it wasn't easy. It was actually so difficult that they all spent one night in jail. Unexpectedly, they were all arrested and taken to jail from a hotel where they had made a stop. Gladys prayed to God every minute that passed, thinking that this was the end of the road for her. She thought that everyone would just get sent back to El Salvador and all her dreams would be flushed down a drain. Her prayers must've been heard, though. The next morning, the guide had a couple of words with the Mexican police and somehow he convinced the police to release the group. Gladys burst into tears and gazed up at the sky with shining eyes as she repeatedly said, "Thank you, Jesus." Nothing could get in Gladys' way now. After a horrible experience of going to jail, nothing could stop her from making her dream come true.

Gladys and the rest of the group finally reached the final border they had to cross. They were at El Rio Bravo dividing Texas and Mexico. Looking at the other side of the river, she felt a huge rush of adrenaline in her body just thinking that she was one final step away from the United States. Everyone began crossing and, while crossing, the war images rushed to her mind. They seemed so real in her head that she thought she could see them clearly in the distance. Before she knew it, she was already stepping on American soil. With their clothes wet and tired, they all walked to a nearby hotel, the "Brownsville" Hotel.

Two days later, a small car drove five people in the group to Raymondville, Texas, and another car drove the other five. The guide went out to speak to other people who were going to help the group finish the rest of the journey. He came back the next morning with a short, skinny man and an old lady in her mid fifties. They split into the groups they had driven to Raymondville with, each led by either the old lady or the skinny man.

Gladys' determination fueled her hopes. The driver of Gladys' group drove the five to a lonely, depressing place, a place which looked as if the people who entered never left, and instead became lost souls. Without anything to eat and hardly anything to drink, the group spent several days and nights walking through the desert. During the daytime, they tried to distance themselves as far as possible from each other. They hid behind bushes so they would not be seen by the immigration agents.

Four days passed and, finally, Gladys' group's guide separated from them because he thought he had seen the other group nearby. He returned with horrible news. Their guide told them that the people he had seen wasn't the other group, it was just other random people who were trying to continue passing into the U.S., just like Gladys and the rest. He told them that they were lost. Gladys' heartbeat accelerated and once again she felt that same feeling, the feeling when she was sent to jail. Huge blows of emotions flowed right through her body. She almost fainted because she believed that this was the end. Immigration would just catch them and send them right back to El Salvador. In desperation, instead of driving out to the road where the immigration station was, she asked the guide to drive them a little closer so that they could barely see the immigration station. She put everything on the line.

The group's guide, with some dismay, did as Gladys told him. He drove them to a safe area where the desert bushes concealed them. Leaving Gladys and the rest of her group on their own, the guide left to the side of the road where immigration, without hesitation, stopped him and sent him back to Mexico.

At night they were left alone. The clouds turned dark and heavy, ready for a downpour, which would play a crucial role. When it began to rain, Gladys and another lady quickly ran to the side of the road to see if someone would pick them up. A couple of cars passed by and didn't stop to pick them up. Gladys and the lady felt hopeless. In their minds they thought that this was the end for them.

Suddenly, they saw a dim light approaching. It got closer and closer very quickly. This is it, Gladys thought. This oncoming car is going to decide for us. If he stops, we are saved, but if he doesn't, we go back to El Salvador. They hugged tightly. When they saw the car was close enough, they jumped, signaling to the car to stop. Miraculously, the car stopped! Quickly, the car pulled over and Gladys and the lady, full of adrenaline, rushed into the car. Filled with happiness and joy, they began to cry.

The driver began to tell Gladys and the other woman how he had once been in the same situation. Gladys couldn't believe how lucky she was to have gotten picked up by this man. She knew she could only go in one direction. She knew how lucky she was that Jesus gave her a second chance. God put an angel in her path: the man who risked his life by stopping in order to provide Gladys a chance at a better life.

Story Of A Young Woman

MARIA URIOSTEGUI

One beautiful afternoon in Cuernavaca, Mexico, a beautiful, young, sixteen-year old woman attended a party at her godmother's home. Her godmother introduced her to a mature man of age twenty-nine. They instantly connected in every way. They giggled and enjoyed each other's presence. Noemi Alquicira was fascinated with this mature older man. While building a relationship with this individual, she felt love in the air and decided to accept his proposal to go out with him.

On a Saturday afternoon, they ate at a taco shop. She thought the food tasted delicious, like a home made meal. Afterwards, while listening to the wonderful sound of falling rain, they waited for a cab. That night, as she slept, she dreamt of one day being married to this wonderful man. Amazed and delighted, she thought that this man would change her life. He had swept her off her feet and helped her with her problems.

Their relationship began like a match made in heaven. Birds sang. She was in love. They could not leave each other's side without missing each other with passion. Whenever they were together, they talked and learned about one another. The relationship progressed amazingly well. Their walks on the beach and in the park became romantic experiences. They showed their affection toward each other by hugging and kissing as if they were the only couple in the world.

He showered her with gifts: teddy bears, chocolates, and flowers. He became her prince who would surprise her with invitations to go to places where she had never gone before. She saw a completely different world. Noemi became dazzled with her new surroundings and new people.

Her new environment consisted of hanging out with an older group of individuals. She felt right at home and enjoyed her time with them. Noemi became fascinated by all the lovely gestures he did for her, like helping her with her problems. For many months the relationship just felt amazing. Whenever she needed help, she ran to him for help. He eased her pain, physical or emotional. He rubbed her feet, massaged her muscles, and spoke to her in an optimistic way to make her feel better. She felt appreciated by her loved one and the love grew until it became enormous. They both said that the relationship would always last no matter the fights and arguments, just as long as the love existed.

When they were not together, they spent hours on the phone and stayed up to hear each other's voices. She had visions of a happy life like a queen's. She believed that her loved one could make this happen. She fell so much in love with her loved one that she could not stay mad at him for long. He had a magical spell on her. He became her sunshine on a rainy day.

In a turn of events, he changed. All of his good gestures were done only to manipulate her in order to achieve his desires. Her vision of him started to change. Her love was gone. She didn't know where it went. His behavior changed in every way and his actions became awkward. He began to mistreat her. The relationship turned from lovely and happy to sad and gloomy. Her feelings were gone. Noemi was in turmoil. She wondered why she fell for this older man. Her feelings were hurt and her future crushed. Noemi left this individual because she realized that all his words, gifts, and help were lies. With a broken heart, she continued with her life. She blocked out the painful memories and tried to live a normal life.

9 Months

BRENDA VALADEZ

It was a warm Monday morning. Margarita's three daughters had already departed to school. She had morning sickness. She suspected the unexpected. She thought that after three daughters she'd be done, but nine years later there she was staring down at a pregnancy test that tested positive.

To make sure the pregnancy test wasn't a mistake, her husband Salvador took her to the clinic on Soto Street. He had missed work to take her. At the clinic the nurse asked her husband, "Do you want to keep the baby?"

Margarita

Obviously, he answered yes. While a dilemma was occurring, Margarita excitedly thought how to tell her daughters. She knew it was too soon to bring their hopes up. Anything could happen in the first few weeks. She decided she would keep it a secret for a while.

It was a Saturday afternoon when she finally decided to tell her daughters. She took Brenda, Cynthia, and Jessica to a fast food restaurant. While they ate, she told them what she'd been hiding.

Cynthia and Jessica lost their appetite and could not even look at the food. Brenda, on the other hand, took the news calmly. She had found out a while back when she found the pregnancy test in the medicine cabinet while she was looking for some tweezers. Margarita's daughters had reacted better than she'd expected.

Margarita was excited after finding out she was pregnant again after nine years. She had forgotten the feeling of finding out one is pregnant. She had forgotten what it felt like to have a baby growing inside you, feeling their little bodies move and kick, and, most importantly, the butterflies a mother gets just thinking about her baby. When she went for a checkup for the second time, she was curious to know whether it was a boy or a girl, but they couldn't tell since the baby had its legs closed. The possibility that she could have a boy made her happy.

A couple of weeks later, Margarita underwent a 3-D ultrasound and the doctors told her it was going to be a baby boy. Her dream of having a boy came true. Margarita would have been happy if it had been a baby girl, but she already had three and a boy was just what she wanted. Her oldest daughter, Brenda, was happy as well. She had known from the beginning that it would be a boy.

Months passed and her belly kept getting bigger. The baby's movements made it harder for Margarita to move around. She could not bend over to pick up stuff from the floor, and even a simple task such as washing the dishes was too much of a load.

Months passed, and Margarita decided it was time to search for the baby's name. She loved the name "Eduardo," but Brenda, who had always said it was going to be a boy, suggested to name him Christopher. Margarita decided she would name him Christopher since she felt it was the right thing to do. Since all her daughters had middle names, Margarita decided Christopher would, too. His middle name would be Jesus since Margarita promised God that if everything went fine throughout the pregnancy, she would give him the name of Jesus. His full name would be Christopher Jesus Valadez; it was the perfect name, she thought.

At eight months her feet began to swell up and she became more and more exhausted. She was at her biggest.

It was between October 2 and October 3 — midnight. Her water broke. She took a shower because Margarita didn't want to smell. She woke up her daughters and told them she was going to the hospital because she was having the baby. When Margarita arrived at White Memorial Hospital she got prepared to have the baby. The baby was born on the morning of October 3, at around eight in the morning. She had her baby boy. She was the happiest she'd been in a long time. She finally had that baby she'd been carrying for nine months in her arms. Christopher Jesus Valadez had been born to fill her life with light.

A Mother's Journey

LUIS VALENCIA

As timed passed, Maria's life became more difficult for her and her husband to handle. Her husband decided to go to the United States to make more money. Soon, she decided to leave her parents to stand beside her beloved husband. In August of 1989, her plans finalized; they hired someone to help them cross the border in order to build a better life for themselves and their newborn daughter.

As they approached the desert near the border, she thought it went on forever. She would have to face many problems and dangers along the way. They waited for the immigration police to change shifts before they made their first move. This happened at one in the morning. When they changed, they started to walk. She thought about her goal of crossing the border. They walked for two hours. During this torturous journey, she took a thirty minute break before they started to walk again.

Maria's brother-in-law Eduardo crossed with them. Everyone knew him because of his heavy drinking. He drank a lot that entire night. He showed signs that he wasn't himself and by the middle of their walk he got up and screamed "Come and get me, immigration!" Everyone grew angry towards him and told him to shut up. Maria got scared about getting caught and the consequences she would face.

As they reached their destination, they saw an entry to a tunnel and realized that their walk was just beginning. Darkness engulfed them; it seemed as if they were walking with their eyes closed. They had to use flashlights to see where they were going. She felt the dirty sewer water up to her neck, and the smell made her gag. She felt scared for her daughters because they might get sick or something worse. After leaving the tunnel, she felt discouraged because they had to walk for long distances.

As time passed, her eyes widened because they finally reached a freeway. It was still not over. They still had to wait for a van heading to Los Angeles. They had to wait for another immigration shift to end so they wouldn't get spotted when the van arrived. The people that she hired to help them cross fed them. She almost drooled as the food was handed to her.

As the time approached, she thought about her parents and how they would have to deal without her, and how she would have to deal without them. She promised her mom she would send them money to help them out with their economic problems.

They saw a van coming full speed. As it got closer, they were told to run as fast as they could towards the van. They climbed over a brick wall in their way. The wall was higher than her shoulder, and she had trouble getting to the other side. Someone rushed her along with her daughter because they couldn't afford to waste any time. Her eyes opened wide and she turned red as the van accelerated full speed. The only reason they got away is that the immigration checkpoint was over and they had the road to themselves. They had to get away as quickly as possible before the border patrol came back and set up another checkpoint. She and the others were relieved that the danger passed and that they were heading for Los Angeles.

She celebrated the success of their journey. They reached her sister-in-law's house. Her heart pounded faster as she saw her husband outside waiting for her to get off. She also felt excited because she heard a lot of positive things about Los Angeles, a place where people could live better lives and achieve any dreams. She wanted to see and to experience everything for herself.

Abdon's Childhood

HORTENCIA VALENZUELA

It was the year of 1968 when Abdon received the shocking news. He was a six-year old boy just wanting to have fun, without any worries. He lived in Mexico, in a town called Tuxpan, Nayarit. He was having the time of his life and was glad to see that his parents were in love with each other, or at least that was what he thought.

One day, Abdon and his little brother, Jesus, were playing in the backyard. Out of the nowhere, they heard screaming coming from inside their house.

"I am tired of this Martha!"

"What do you mean, Abdon? I have not done nothing wrong!"

"I have decided to leave you!"

"What, you can't leave me here alone with two kids!"

Abdon and his brother decided to check out what was going on, but they were too young to understand why it was that their parents were talking so loudly. They just stood there, staring from behind the door, wondering what their parents were doing.

The arguing went on for a while. Both Abdon and his brother had puzzled faces, wondering what was going on and whether or not they should just enter the room. All of a sudden, out of nowhere, they saw their father coming out of the room with a suitcase, heading for the door. They wondered where he was going. Once he was gone, both Abdon and his little brother went inside the room and saw that their mother was crying on the bed. They approached her and Abdon asked his mother why she was crying. His mother Martha replied that their father had gone away. Six year-old Abdon thought she meant that his father had gone away on vacation. So to make his mother feel better, he started telling her, "Don't worry mom, dad will come back soon." Just from hearing those words, Martha started to cry even harder, so he decided to hug her. Later on, his mother told both Abdon and Jesus to go and play outside, and they did as their mother told them to do. Later on, the mother started wondering what she was going to do about her money situation.

The next day, she went to visit her father and brother. She told them how her husband had walked out on her. Martha's father and brother felt devastated and shocked by the news, and decided to help her with her money problems and with raising her two children. After a while, Martha found a job in Tijuana, and she had to leave her two sons for a while and would be gone the whole day. Every time Abdon saw his mother leaving, he told her not to go and to stay with them, but there was nothing she could do but just walk away crying. Abdon did not understand why his mother would leave each day and for so long. Martha would not tell her sons why she could not stay with them because they were too young to understand how she had to leave to work in Tijuana to earn the money to feed and clothe them.

After that, Abdon and Jesus never worried about what they were going to eat. They always ate eggs, beans, chicken, and other things. At that time, Abdon was too young to realize that his father was never coming back. His mother became a strong woman because of what had happened to her, and in order to help support her two kids, because Abdon's father did not give them any money at all.

As the years passed, Abdon's mother ended up having two more kids. As Abdon and his brothers got older, he started realizing why his father had left. It was because his parents argued too much and felt that they no longer got along as well as they used to, and because his father no longer loved his mother. To this day, he still does not know exactly why his father left them on that day. But one thing was for sure, growing up without a father affected him. He felt resentment towards his father for just leaving him and for not being with him as he was growing up. At the same time, this experience made Abdon a better person. Once he overcame the fact that he grew up without a father, he himself became a better father with his daughters, and vowed to never do such a thing as his father once did forty-three years ago.

The Road To Education

JOHN VARGAS

A woman named Lorena Villaurrutia began her life well. She lived with both her parents. Free of problems, she thought everything was going well. However, when she was around eight years old, she was unwillingly sent to her brother's house where she would begin her new life. Seven people lived in their household, including Lorena, her brother, his wife and his four kids.

Lorena Villaurrutia

The kids and the father were nice and courteous towards her, but the mom was a real pain in the butt. She hassled her and forced her to do jobs around the house. Lorena didn't know she would become a maid who would cook, clean dishes, clean the house, and babysit children, without any pay. She did all this while in school. At times, she would not even finish her school assignments because of all the things she needed to finish at home. She could not rebel because she knew that once she did, she would be severely punished. They didn't even care about her; therefore, her self-esteem decreased greatly.

At one point, when she was cooking a desert, she was burned by the sugar and didn't know what to do, but she did know that she was not going to tell anyone in the house about what had just happened. The skin on her hand was peeling off. Her brother's wife saw the burn, but completely ignored it.

Lorena did not even eat nutritiously. Food at the school was provided, but she had no money to purchase the food. She did not even have full meals. Her brother's wife made shakes for the children, but she did not have enough milk to make a shake for Lorena. She just poured water in the mixer and poured it in a cup for her. She was forced to drink it even though it tasted nasty. This would be the only meal she would have for the day since she was never given any money.

After all the pain and torture, Lorena set off to college to become a business major. She began to realize that without all the events she had gone through, she would have not been at college at this point in life. She realized that her experiences would help her in the future. But now, she faced financial problems in college because her parents only paid for the tuition and not for her other needs, such as food and clothing. When she finished college, she started work at an IRS building in Mexico.

American Dream

MIGUEL VARGAS

My father lived with my mom, Guadalupe, in his parents' attic. They lived in a terrible community, but had a decent house. My father was very grateful for the house where he lived, but he wanted more. He didn't want his family living in a broken down old shack; he wanted a place he could call home.

My father had one goal in life—to give his family a decent life. He figured being in his hometown of Leon Guanajuato wouldn't get him very far, so he decided to look for a better opportunity. He had overheard a couple of guys talking about how they could cross people over the border to the United States. My father was aware that while crossing the border, many people wouldn't make it across and might remain stranded in the desert and never make it out. He knew that if he intended to cross he would either make it across or he would stay in the desert permanently and not be able to help his family at all. He knew that by trying to cross the desert he was putting his life in danger. It was a risk he was willing to take.

It was November 12, 1991, when my father went to speak to my grandparents. He went to say his goodbyes to both of his parents. He tried to explain to my grandpa that the only reason he was doing this was because of his family. His mom couldn't bear it. She couldn't accept the fact that my dad was leaving and that it would be the last time she saw him. As my dad turned to give my grandma her goodbye hug, she gave him her back and held back no tears.

She said, "When you leave, please don't say goodbye because it will be the last time we see each other."

My father's whole body shivered. His watery eyes tried to hold back emotions. He told them he would leave at 7:00 pm. When the time came, my dad started saying his goodbyes again to everyone in his family except his mom. As he walked out the door, he turned and, without a single word, glanced back and slowly walked behind her. He gave her a kiss on her beautiful burgundy hair and walked out of his parents' home. With no words spoken, he and his mom didn't sustain their tears. He understood why she did what she did. She hated watching her youngest child leave forever; it was too much pain for her to handle.

That night, my father headed for the United States. Fifteen other people and he traveled together as a pack. They were led by a single "coyote". When they reached the desert it was night time. It was dark and lonely. It got colder every minute. It was very frightening because at every corner danger lurked. The only light they had was the moon shining over them. My dad's adrenaline was up the whole time; he had fear in his eyes, as did everyone else.

"It's going to be a long night," the coyote said. It felt like an eternity to my father. When morning came my father understood why the coyote had made that comment. It turned out they were lost and were rapidly running out of water and food. My dad tried to keep positive thoughts about his plight, but his heart pounded harder than a piston in an engine.

After two long days of walking, they ran out of food and water. They were getting desperate. The coyote told them that it was only a bit farther to freedom. My father started feeling drowsy. He felt he wasn't going to make it, so he just sat there under a cactus where there was a bit of shade. His lips and tongue were turning dry white; his feet were too heavy for him. As he lay there in the cactus shade feeling alone, he thought about his family, and how he had failed them. As he sat there praying and hoping that he wouldn't stay there permanently, he felt a drop of water fall onto his forehead. He was speechless, filled with hope. Slowly, he rose to his feet and with the help of two other men, they cut a hole in the cactus, which contained water. They each took a sip and my father said it was the most delicious water he ever tasted. He believed that he had gotten his second opportunity in life.

Remembering The Old Times

EDGAR VELEZ

Antonio

On a beautiful morning, Antonio woke up from a soft and comfortable bed, which he liked because he had worked six days in a row. He wanted to continue sleeping because he was tired of working so much at a "Tortilleria," still his only job since he came to the United States. When Antonio arrived for the first time, he thought that the USA would be a better place to live, with a lot more opportunities than back home in Mexico.

He found a place where he could start working, a tortilleria named "Romero's," like other individuals do when they arrive, even if they don't like the work. Since he was an immigrant and it was his first time touching new land, he didn't have the same opportunities as a U.S. citizen. This business was the first job that he found and the one that hired him without any documentation.

That morning, he didn't want to get up to eat because he was so tired. Antonio, who had been fat since he was a little kid, liked to eat, especially when his wife Maria cooked meat. He heard his daughters, Kimberly and Natalie. Natalie, the youngest, screamed "Papa!" to him. They both looked a lot like him; they both had the same face and were chubby like him. He loved them so much. When he woke up to get his little girl, he saw his daughter Kimberly playing her Nintendo DS. As he watched them, he began to remember his childhood, how he used to live, and how he used to struggle in life with his family. He always wanted to have a video game, but he never had money to afford one.

As he was sitting down on his bed with his little girl Natalie on his arms, he pictured himself living a poverty stricken life. He remembered eating "frijoles" every day. It was the only food they could afford in those times. If his family wanted to buy some kind of meat, it would cost them more. He had no schooling, and he didn't like studying, writing, or reading. He preferred the fields, working under the rays of the sun, with the hot air touching his face, and with his entire body sweating. Since his clothes and shoes were not in good condition, he was embarrassed that the kids at school would make fun of him for being poor and for using a plastic bag as a backpack. For him, there was no shower. He didn't know the word clean; he preferred to be dirty.

His eyes began to show anger. He remembered his own dad, who had never wanted to give money to his kids for school. In Mexico, the students needed to buy their lunch, like a "torta" and a juice, and he never received the money from his dad to buy his lunch. His father was also an alcoholic who liked to drink a lot with his friends and waste his money on beer. He was in the habit of drinking after getting his check. He always ended up paying for everyone's "Coronitas." Antonio's mother, however, always worked hard. She had to make tortillas and sell them to the neighbors. It was a hard job. She had to get up at 5:00 a.m. every day to make them natural and delicious. Even during the hard times, she didn't give up until she had some food to give to her kids.

As his little girl was playing, he thought about the time when his father didn't let him go out with his friends and have fun. Antonio remembered his past with such sadness that he didn't want to go back. He never wanted to relive those times again.

Suddenly, Antonio's wife startled him back to reality when she started calling him and their daughters to the kitchen to go eat. As she entered the room, she noticed that Antonio was kind of lost and sad.

She asked him, "What happened?"

He didn't answer, but just simply nodded. He realized that what had happened to him was in the past. It would stay in his memory, but he would choose to live in the present and enjoy his new life, watching his girls grow up. He gave each of his girls a hug and kissed them. He took them to the table so they could eat as a family. Together, they enjoyed the food that his wife had cooked for him and his little girls.

Story Of A Girl

IGNACIO ZERMENO

Mexico City in 1978. During summertime, people left their hot, uncomfortable homes. Little boys and girls played with the broken water pumps to stay cool and wet. Neighbors talked to other neighbors as if they were a family — that was called a "vecindad" or "la cuadra."

Velazquez and her family enjoyed their time outside. Laughing with one another and eating carne asada while watching their soccer games, they told their own life stories and the problems that they had faced once. Around the corner, Rosa's brothers smoked and threw up their gang sign. They wanted to get youngsters to join their gang. They did not care who it was or what age. They just wanted to make it bigger and wanted power over the "Barrio."

Late that night, Rosa met up with her brother at the same spot. She was ready to get jumped in. She did not know what awaited her. It was pure, fresh danger. When Rosa turned the corner, gunshots fired. She dropped to the floor, barely dodging a bullet. Getting up, she saw her brother Temo lying on the cold concrete floor. She closed her eyes and repeated to herself, "No, No, No!"

Rosa ran home to her family to give them the news. Everyone broke down in tears; their faces were full of shock. Rosa ran into her room, broke down in tears, and stayed in her black hole. Seven days later, Rosa went back to the streets to kick it with the same people who hung out with her brother. Even though Rosa didn't do drugs, she was around dangerous people. Her life was at risk constantly.

Rosa learned the meaning of life when she lost her second brother in a gunfight: three shots to the body and one shot straight through the skull. Confused, Rosa didn't know what to think or what to do. She was still in her black hole that she couldn't escape. She struggled for a long period of time.

One day she managed to escape that black hole. Rosa's way of thinking changed to one that was more positive. No more gangs, no more being around the wrong friends, no more drugs. She wanted to set an example for her kids. She wanted to have a story to tell her children about what happened and why her life changed.

Our Hopes and Dreams

Ismael Aguiar: My hopes and dreams are to become the first person in my family to go to college and to set an example for my younger brother.

Reina Aguirre: I hope that my loved ones will have good health and that someday I will have a great career.

Wendy Aguirre: My hopes and dreams are to go to college and to become an OB-GYN.

Aracely Alvarado: My hopes are to help people and to be happy.

Xochilt Alvarez: I aspire to be a better person in terms of education and morals, to continue to be consistent, and to practice what I learn daily to achieve a better future.

Jesus Arellano: My hopes and dreams are to become a firefighter for the city full time.

Arturo Banda: My hopes and dreams are to get a good career and to have a better future.

Melanie Barajas: My hopes and dreams are to graduate from UCSB with my B.A. in Political Science, to transfer to USC for my Ph.D. in Politics, and to become the Mayor of Los Angeles.

Allan Bautista: My dreams are to stay in touch with my parents and to become a good mechanical engineer.

Rebecca Baxter: My hopes and dreams are about breaking the cycle of parenting alone, and ultimately about giving my child a better life than previously lived before him.

Alejandro Berumen: My hopes and dreams are to become a firefighter.

Juan Carbajal: My biggest goal in life is to be famous and to be a published author, one down, one to go.

Magdalena Ceja: I hope to graduate UCLA but keep attending school with the ultimate goal of attaining a Ph.D.

Karen Cerezo: To live life to the fullest with everyone, and to achieve and overcome difficulties in life.

Omar Cruz: I hope to attend a four-year university, to play professional soccer, and to own an art studio.

Michelle Duran: My hopes and dreams are to live life to the fullest, with much happiness and love.

Leslie Escobedo: I hope that someday I'll become a psychologist.

Agustin Esparza: My hopes and dreams are to enter the field of criminal justice and to get back to my parents.

Elizabeth Farafan: My life ambition is to go big or nothing at all, no fear, and live life as much as I could.

Denise Felix: My hopes and dreams are to travel the world in a year.

Edgar Garcia: My hopes and dreams are to transfer from community college and major in social services; I hope I can die an old man to live life and watch my children grow.

Isabel Garcia: I don't want to be famous, but to be known for my success.

Stephanie Gonzales: My hopes and dreams are to graduate from a four year university and get my Ph.D.

Miguel Hernandez: I hope to go to college and graduate, and I dream of owning a beautiful house, surrounded by a wonderful family.

Justo Juarez: My hopes and dreams are to receive a B.A by the age of twenty three and, if possible, move on to a Master's degree.

Michelle Lira: My dreams and hopes are that hatred of all bisexual, lesbian, and gay people ends.

Nancy Lopez: My hopes and dreams are to help people understand that for every negative issue there is also a brighter side to it as well.

Nicholas Manriquez: My dream is to become what I want and to make my family proud.

Alyssa Medina: My hopes and dreams are to become the best person I can be and to be successful in every aspect of life.

Marissa Medina: My hopes and dreams are to finish college and to be happy with myself and the way my life has turned out due to my hard work, determination, honor, and integrity.

Oscar Mojica: I hope to attend college and to be the next President of the United States.

Lesly Molina: My dream is to become an activist and to overcome challenges to suppressing racism.

Betty Morales: I hope to help people in need and to be helped when I am in need.

Jesus Oropeza: My hopes and dreams after high school are to find a job to support my needs and to attend ELAC.

Angelica Ortega: I hope and dream for the day the Dream Act passes and undocumented students receive financial aid.

Hector Ortega: My hopes and dreams are to finish school and everything else that deals with school. I just want to work and see where life takes me.

Georgina Portillo: My hope is to reach my dream of having a career, family, a place to call home, and a story to remember.

Julio Prado: I hope to see my failures as a healthy, inevitable part of the process of becoming successful.

Maribel Ramon: No one said life will be easy, I hope that every senior accomplishes their goals and dreams.

Anthony Romo: I dream to have a good income, a master's degree, and the ability to help my family.

Adriana Salas: My hopes and dreams are to graduate from Stanford and to become a psychologist.

Michelle Salinas: My hopes and dreams include finding a career where I can continue to fight for social justice across the globe.

David Sanchez: My hope and dream for my future is to be able to help others.

Juan Sibrian: I hope for a better future and dream of a wealthy life.

Eduardo Simental: My hopes and dreams are to make people understand that people will always have problems no matter how grave it is. You just have to find the right way to cope with it without harming yourself.

Esthefanie Solano: I aspire to make my life dream come true by obtaining my doctorate and practicing medicine as a pediatrician for underserved communities.

Joseph Torres: My hopes and dreams are to become a firefighter.

Cristian Umanzor: My hope is for the next rising generation to be more dedicated to school than my generation. My dream is to one day carry on my own family.

Maria Uriostegui: My hopes and dreams are to shine like a star in the sky, and help the ones in need.

Brenda Valadez: I want to do something that matters, to say something different, and to leave nothing less than something that says I was here.

Luis Valencia: My dream is to have a good successful life.

Hortencia Valenzuela: My hopes and dreams for the future is for the economy to get better.

John Vargas: My hopes and dreams are to realize what I really want to achieve in life.

Miguel Vargas: My hopes and dreams are to give my family the life they have always struggled to achieve.

Edgar Velez: My hopes are for all the world to be the same, yet beautiful; my dream is to die one day, but live forever.

Ignacio Zermeno: My hopes and dreams are to become a professional soccer player by the age of 23, and to major in criminology and law enforcement.

~

The Writers

Acknowledgments

Special Thanks for Funding and Support:

FEDCO Charitable Foundation
Kaz and Linda Kishimoto
Cynthia Gonzalez, Principal, School of Law and Government
Sandra Lopez, Counselor, School of Law and Government
Teacher Editors: Monica Yoo, Ashley Englander, Leticia Carlos, Danny Melendez, Eddie Lopez, Carlos Castillo, Deborah Chapman

***

The following students of the Class of 2011, School of Law and Government at Roosevelt High School, assumed key responsibilities for the editing, design, and layout of the book: Magdalena Ceja, Adylene Gonzalez, Esthefanie Solano, Melanie Barajas, Michelle Salinas, Jesus Gonzalez, Karen Cerezo, Marissa Medina, Michelle Lira, Eddie Ruiz

***

Project Directed and Coordinated by:
Jeffrey Matsumura, English Teacher
Leticia Rojas, English Teacher
Steve Mereu, Collaborative Teacher

This book is part of In Our Global Village (IOGV), a global service learning program, an invitation for student participation in a collaborative exchange of global stories to a worldwide community. Initiated in response to In Our Village, a book written by students of Awet Secondary School in Kambi ya Simba, Tanzania, IOGV was founded as a partnership between Cathryn Berger Kaye, CBK Associates, and Barbara Cervone, What Kids Can Do.

For more information, to join the In Our Global Village process, and to see books written by students in countries all over the world, please visit www.inourvillage.org. Click on the In Our Global Village Project link.

We also invite you to learn more about each of our partners:
    CBK Associates at *www.abcdbooks.org*
    What Kids Can Do at *www.whatkidscando.org*

www.ingramcontent.com/pod-product-compliance
Lightning Source LLC
Chambersburg PA
CBHW061649040426
42446CB00010B/1652